Anne of France:
Lessons for my Daughter

Library of Medieval Women   ISSN 1369–9652

Series Editor: Jane Chance

The Library of Medieval Women aims to make available, in an English translation, significant works by, for, and about medieval women, from the age of the Church Fathers to the fifteenth century. The series encompasses many forms of writing, from poetry, visions, biography and autobiography, and letters, to sermons, treatises and encyclopedias; the subject matter is equally diverse: theology and mysticism, classical mythology, medicine and science, history, hagiography, and instructions for anchoresses. Each text is presented with an introduction setting the material in context, a guide to further reading, and an interpretive essay.

We welcome suggestions for future titles in the series. Proposals or queries may be sent directly to the editor or publisher at the addresses given below; all submissions will receive prompt and informed consideration.

Professor Jane Chance, Department of English, MS 30, Rice University, PO Box 1892, Houston, TX 77251–1892, USA. E-mail: jchance@rice.edu

Boydell & Brewer Limited, PO Box 9, Woodbridge, Suffolk, IP12 3DF, UK. E-mail: editorial@boydell.co.uk. Website: www.boydellandbrewer.com

Previously published titles in this series are listed at the back of this book

Anne of France:
Lessons for my Daughter

Translated from the French
with Introduction, Notes and Interpretive Essay

Sharon L. Jansen

D.S. BREWER

First published 2004
D. S. Brewer, Cambridge

ISBN 1 84384 016 2

D. S. Brewer is an imprint of Boydell & Brewer Ltd
PO Box 9, Woodbridge, Suffolk IP12 3DF, UK
and of Boydell & Brewer Inc.
PO Box 41026, Rochester, NY 41026–4126, USA
website: www.boydellandbrewer.com

A catalogue record for this book is available
from the British Library

Library of Congress Cataloging-in-Publication Data
Anne, of France, 1461–1522.
  [Enseignements d'Anne de France, duchesse de Bourbonnais et d'Auvergne, à sa fille
  Suzanne de Bourbon. English]
  Anne of France : lessons for my daughter / translated from the French, with introduction,
  notes and interpretive essay.
    p. cm. – (Library of medieval women, ISSN 1369–9652)
  Includes bibliographical references and index.
  ISBN 1–84384–016–2 (Hardback : alk. paper)
  1. Conduct of life–Early works to 1800.   2. Christian life–Early works to 1800.
I. Jansen, Sharon L., 1951-II. Title.   III. Series.
  BJ1552.A5613 2004
  170′.44–dc22   2003025369

This publication is printed on acid-free paper

Printed in Great Britain by
Antony Rowe Ltd, Chippenham, Wiltshire

Contents

For my dear friend Georgina Burlingame, with my deepest appreciation for the years of friendship we have shared. As Anne of France says, "in prosperity you will find friends enough, but in adversity, few."

Preface

In *A Room of One's Own*, Virginia Woolf suggested that "we think back through our mothers if we are women." I found myself remembering her words as I began translating Anne of France's lessons for her daughter, Suzanne of Bourbon. The process was a strangely intimate one: slowly, word by word, sometimes even letter by letter, I was deciphering the admonitions, advice, and warnings a fifteenth-century princess directed to her daughter, all the while and against all logic hearing my own mother's voice in my mind. And then one day, midway through the process of turning French into English, I looked away from my pile of dictionaries to the framed portraits of Anne and Suzanne that sat on the desk where I was working.[1] Studying their faces, I knew I had to find the quotation that I remembered.

I did find it, about three-quarters of the way through the slim volume, as Woolf was describing the struggle of women writers. Although they were confronted by "discouragement and criticism," Woolf wrote, "that was unimportant compared with the other difficulty which faced them . . . when they came to set their thoughts on paper—that is that they had no tradition behind them, or one so short and partial that it was of little help." And then the sentence: "For we think back through our mothers if we are women."[2]

Anne of France's text seems at first to challenge Woolf's claim, for in composing a series of lessons for her daughter, Anne *did* have a tradition of women behind her, and a rather long one. As she wrote, she could "think back" to Christine de Pizan's *The Treasure of the City of Ladies*, written a hundred years earlier, a book that Anne had owned and read, a book that, in fact, she had inherited from her mother, Charlotte of Savoy, queen of France. And, although Anne addressed her lessons to her daughter, she clearly came to see herself contributing to the tradition she inherited, since her book was passed on to other daughters of other mothers: her lessons were published

---

[1] Portraits of Anne of France and her daughter, painted by John Hey (the Master of Moulins), can be viewed at two on-line galleries: http://gallery.euroweb. hu/html/m/master/moulins and http://cgfa.sunsite.dk/hey/index.html.

[2] Virginia Woolf, *A Room of One's Own* (New York: Harvest, 1989), 76.

"at the request" of Suzanne, doubtless with her mother's approval.[3] This first edition, printed between 1517 and 1521, was followed by a second printing in 1534.[4] A third edition was published the next year, this time dedicated to Marguerite of Angoulême, a daughter of another powerful mother, Louise of Savoy, and herself the mother of Jeanne d'Albret, who would become queen regnant of Navarre.[5]

But, despite the status of Anne of France and her daughter Suzanne, and despite the fact that the book went through three editions within thirty years of its composition, her work disappeared. The tradition she had inherited was also lost—Christine de Pizan's *Treasure of the City of Ladies*, composed in 1405 and widely circulated in manuscript, was printed in Paris in 1497, 1503, and 1536, but, in the words of Sarah Lawson, who published the first translation of Christine's work in English, "by the seventeenth century hardly anyone had heard of her."[6]

---

[3]   A single copy of this printed edition survives and is now in the rare book room of the Bibliothèque nationale de France, Paris (Réserve D. 80044). The title page of the small volume, printed in Lyons with no date, reads: "At the request of . . . Suzanne of Bourbon . . . daughter of Anne of France" (my translation). For a full description of the book, see Henri Baudrier, *Bibliographie Lyonnaise: Recherches sur les imprimeurs, libraires, relieurs et fondeurs de lettres de Lyon au xvie siècle*, 2d ser., vol. 12 (Lyon, France: F. Brossier, 1921), 159–60.

[4]   The Baudrier catalogue (12:160) notes that the elongated form of the printed book was introduced in 1517, thus establishing the earliest date for the book's publication. Suzanne of Bourbon died in April 1521; to have been printed "at her request," the book must have been printed before that date. On the date of publication, see "Introduction," 16.

    A single copy of the second edition, "newly printed" (*imprimée nouuellement*) by Claude Nourry, is also in the Bibliothèque nationale (Department of Western Manuscripts, Rothschild Collection No. 2559); for a full description, see Émile Picot, *Catalogue des livres composant la bibliothèque de feu M. le baron James de Rothschild* (Paris: Damascène Morgand, 1893), 3:354–55. For the date, I am grateful to Nicolas Petit, Conservateur à la Réserve des livres rares, Bibliothèque nationale de France.

[5]   Marguerite of Angoulême (b. 1492) married Henry d'Albret, king of Navarre, in 1527. Her mother, Louise of Savoy (1476–1531), was twice regent of France for her son Francis I, Marguerite's brother. Marguerite's daughter, Jeanne d'Albret (b. 1528), inherited the throne of Navarre in 1555, ruling until her death in 1572.

    The 1535 edition of Anne of France's book, printed in Toulouse by Eustace Mareschal, was dedicated to the "most illustrious and powerful princess and lady, Madam Marguerite of France, queen of Navarre"; two copies survive, one in the Bibliothèque nationale (Department of Western Manuscripts, Rothschild Collection No. 2754) and one in the British Library, London (No. 8415.d.9). For a full description, see Picot, 4:26–28.

[6]   Sarah Lawson, trans., *Christine de Pisan: The Treasure of the City of Ladies; or, The Book of the Three Virtues* (New York: Penguin Books, 1985), 15. The first edition in

We almost surely would not be able to "think back" to Anne's text today were it not for the work of one man, a nineteenth-century scholar named A. M. Chazaud.[7] Chazaud never tells us how or why or when he became interested in Anne's lessons for her daughter— it's not even clear that he knew of the existence of her work before he traveled from France to the Hermitage Museum in St. Petersburg. As archivist of the department of Allier, formed from the old province of Bourbonnais, he may have gone to the Hermitage to work with a manuscript of the chronicles of Louis I, first duke of Bourbon; Chazaud returned to France to publish an edition of that fifteenth-century text in 1876.[8] Whether or not he knew about Anne's work before he arrived in St. Petersburg, while there he transcribed not only the chronicles of the duke of Bourbon but her text; he added an introduction, appended a discussion of her language, compiled a glossary, and published *Les Enseignements d'Anne de France . . . à sa fille Susanne de Bourbon* in 1878.[9]

French since 1536 is Charity Cannon Willard and Eric Hicks, eds., *Christine de Pizan: Le Livre des trois vertus* (Paris: Librairie Honoré Champion, 1989).

[7] Information about Chazaud (b. 1827) is somewhat confused. Although the title page of his edition of Anne's *enseignements* clearly prints his name as "A.-M. Chazaud," several sources reverse the initials as "M. A." (The on-line catalogue of the Bibliothèque nationale, for example, uses both "A. M." and "M. A." for different copies of the same book.) The BN on-line catalogue also variously refers to him as "Alphonse Martial" and "Martial-Alphonse."

[8] In his edition of Anne's lessons, Chazaud notes (241n.) that he worked on the manuscript of the chronicles while he was in St. Petersburg, publishing *La Chronicle du bon duc Loys de Bourbon* (Paris: Librarie Renouard) on his return to France.

[9] (Moulins: C. Desrosiers). Chazaud died two years later, in 1880. Chazaud's edition was reprinted in Marseille by Laffitte Reprints in 1978 (an edition limited to 500 copies).

In his edition Chazaud also prints a text entitled *Extrait d'une espitre consolatoire transmise à une dame nommée Katerine de Neufville, dame de Frène, sur la mort et trespas de son premier et seul filz . . .* [Extract from a Consolatory Epistle Sent to a Lady Named Katherine de Neufville, Lady of Fresne, on the Death and Passing Away of Her First and Only Son . . .], which he found bound together with the manuscript of Anne's *enseignements.* He assumes that this second text, which he discusses only briefly (xxxiv–xxxix), is also by Anne of France, though this second text is not discussed (or even mentioned) by Gustave Bertrand, *Catalogue des manuscrits français de la Bibliothèque de Saint-Petersbourg* (Paris: Imprimerie Nationale, 1874), 96 or by Alexandre de Laborde, *Les principaux manuscripts à peintures conservés dans l'ancienne Bibliothèque imperiale publique de Saint-Pétersbourg* (Paris: Pour les membres de la Société française de reproductions de manuscrits à peintures, 1938), 2:142–44. Since there is no study of this second text that I am aware of, and no evidence offered for attributing it to Anne of France, I am not sure that we should assume her authorship. Further study remains to be done.

While he does not tell us how he came to edit Anne's text, Chazaud does explain how the book that Anne had given her daughter came to be in Russia, for the manuscript he found there was, in fact, Suzanne's own copy of the book: *Ce livre est à moy, Susanne de Bourbon, et l'ey eu de la meson de Bourbon* was written on the first folio.[10] The story of the manuscript's journey from France to St. Petersburg is fascinating, and starting from the information Chazaud supplies, we can fill in a few more details of the manuscript's odyssey. After the death of Suzanne's husband in 1527, the Bourbon library became the property of King Francis I and was transferred from the library of Moulins to Fontainebleu. Later, the manuscript was a gift to Diane de Poitiers, who had been educated by Anne of France, and it became part of the library at her chateau of Anet.[11] Two brief notes in the manuscript indicate that on "the last day of the month and year of 1632" a certain Monsieur Baillet de Sainte-Barbe from the town of Dreux gave the book to an unnamed but very happy recipient who lived on Chantre street in Paris; once in Paris, the manuscript passed to the library of Pierre Séguier, chancellor of France under kings Louis XIII and Louis XIV.[12] From the library of the chancellor, the book passed to his grandson, Henri-Charles du Cambout de Coislin, bishop of Metz, and from him to the library of the abbey of Saint-Germain-des-Prés.[13] In 1791, in the midst of the French Revolution, some fifty of the Saint-Germain manuscripts were acquired by a Russian diplomat, Peter Dubrovsky, who was in Paris purchasing books for Catherine II, empress of Russia, and, ultimately, for his own growing collection.[14] Anne's

---

[10] "This book is mine, Susanne of Bourbon, and it comes from (literally 'I have had it from') the house of Bourbon" (Chazaud, iii). Chazaud transcribes all the writing on the flyleaves (iii–v) and includes hand-drawn facsimiles; his edition also includes copies of the manuscript's miniatures, which he attributed to Mathurin Louis Armand Queyroy, *passim*.

[11] Diane de Poitiers (1499–1566) was not only raised by Anne of France, but her marriage to Louis of Brézé was also arranged by Anne; after her husband's death in 1521 Diane became the mistress of Henry II of France, son of Francis I, who probably presented her with the manuscript. There is no indication when she received the gift or when the manuscript left her library at Anet.

[12] For the notes made by the unnamed recipient of the book, see Chazaud, vi–vii; Dreux is in the department of Eure-et-Loir, as is the chateau of Anet. Pierre de Séguier (b. 1588) became chancellor of France in 1635 and died in 1672, so that provides some indication of when he might have owned the book.

[13] Henry Charles de Coislin (1665–1732) bequeathed his library to the abbey.

[14] Chazaud is specific about the date of 1791 (vii), but it is not mentioned by Laborde, who does discuss the manuscript's provenance (2:143). Catherine the Great (1729–96) became empress of Russia in 1762.

manuscript was among Dubrovsky's acquisitions; in 1805, it was transferred to the Imperial Public Library.[15]

And there it remained, at least for a time. The few scholars who have written about Anne's text have assumed that the manuscript is still there, preserved for us, waiting for us to pick it up and touch the very pages that Suzanne turned as she read her mother's words.[16] But the manuscript is there no longer—it was sold at some during the 1930s, and its current location, if it still exists, is unknown.[17]

For information on Peter Dubrovsky, see Patricia Z. Thompson, "Biography of a Library: The Western European Manuscript Collection of Peter P. Dubrovskii in Leningrad," *The Journal of Library History* 9 (1984), 477–503 and T. P. Voronova, "P. P. Dubrovskiî, 1754–1816, and the Saint-Germain Manuscripts," *The Book Collector* 27.4 (1978), 469–78. The Thompson essay is particularly valuable for its discussion of the devastating impact of the Revolution on French libraries and archives.

[15] For the specific date the manuscript came into the possession of the Imperial Public Library, I am indebted to A. P. Romanov, Chief of Foreign Acquisitions, National Library of Russia, personal letter, 22 July 2002. Romanov's letter may also provide a clue as to when Chazaud transcribed Anne's text. Chazaud indicates (i) that the manuscript is at the Hermitage; according to Romanov, the manuscript (then catalogued as MS. Fr. Q.v.III.2) remained at the Imperial Public Library from its receipt until 1849, when a group of illuminated manuscripts was transferred to the Hermitage Museum as part of a display. The manuscripts stayed there until 1861 when, Romanov writes, "all illuminated manuscripts were returned from the Hermitage to the Public Library." Since Chazaud states that the manuscript he saw was at the Hermitage, it seems likely that he was in Russia between 1849 and 1861.

[16] See, for example, Charity Cannon Willard, "Anne de France, Reader of Christine de Pizan," in *The Reception of Christine de Pizan from the Fifteenth through the Nineteenth Centuries: Visitors to the City*, ed. Glenda K. McLeod (Lewiston, NY: The Edwin Mellen Press, 1991), 59; Roberta L. Krueger, "*Chascune selon son estat*: Women's Education and Social Class in the Conduct Books of Christine de Pizan and Anne de France," *Papers on French Seventeenth Century Literature* 24.46 (1997), 25; and, most recently, Pauline Matarasso, *Queen's Mate: Three Women of Power in France on the Eve of the Renaissance* (Burlington, VT: Ashgate Publishing, 2001), 196 n. 22.

[17] According to Romanov, the manuscript was sold "through the 'Antiquary,'" which was either "an antique store or an auction"; the library knows "nothing about its location." One further query produced a confirmation from the Institut de Recherche et d'Histoire des Textes (Centre Nationale de la Recherche), Section de l'Humanism (Paris), indicating that nothing further is known of the manuscript, but holding out the hope that "with luck" it may perhaps be found someday (personal communication, 17 January 2003).

In his description of the manuscript, Laborde indicates that Suzanne's handwriting is "very faded" (*très effaces*), suggesting that he was working directly from the manuscript itself, since Chazaud does not make this point. Laborde also disagrees quite strongly with Chazaud's assessment of the miniatures, calling

And so, in the end, Anne of France's book seems to illustrate rather than to challenge Woolf's view that the "tradition" women have inherited is a fragmented and disrupted one. Like so many medieval texts, the survival of her work seems entirely a matter of chance—passed from hand to hand, the manuscript copy of her lessons also passed through more than four centuries of disaster, war, and revolution, only to be sold and then to disappear. And yet, despite the odds, her text *did* survive—one copy of the first printed edition, one of the second, two of the third, and, luckily, a careful edition of the manuscript itself, made before its disappearance. Chazaud's 1878 edition, which itself survives in only a handful of copies, was reprinted in 1978, ensuring that Anne's lessons could be passed on to a generation of scholars intent on recovering women's history and enabling them, in Woolf's words, to begin rewriting the "short and partial" tradition they inherited.[18] From Anne of France to Suzanne of Bourbon to Diane de Poitiers to Catherine the Great to us.

We have also inherited a tradition of scholarly work on this text, from Chazaud himself in the nineteenth century, to Alice Hentsch and Joseph Viple early in the twentieth, to Colette Winn and Diane Bornstein in the 1980s, and then to Charity Cannon Willard and Roberta Krueger in the 1990s.[19] Pauline Matarasso's *Queen's Mate: Three Women of Power in France on the Eve of the Renaissance*, published in 2001, contains the first extended biographical treatment of Anne of France in English.[20]

I first learned of Anne of France's text from Constance Jordan's *Renaissance Feminism: Literary Texts and Political Models*.[21] Jordan's brief but intriguing analysis of Anne's lessons sent me first to Chazaud and led, ultimately, to the edition printed here as part of Boydell and Brewer's Library of Medieval Women. I would like to thank those who have helped make this edition possible, particularly

---

them "very bad," "weak imitations" of the work of painters who Chazaud suggested might have executed them (144).

[18] The Online Computer Library Center (OCLC) WorldCat, which lists the holdings of 43,559 libraries in 86 countries, notes fewer than a dozen copies of Chazaud's edition. In 1955, the authors of a biography of Anne of France commented that Chazaud's edition had become nearly impossible to find; see Hedwige de Chabannes and Isabelle de Linarès, *Anne de Beaujeu: "Ce fut ung roy"* (Paris: Crépin-Leblond, 1955), 141.

[19] For these critical studies, see "Introduction," n. 43.

[20] See "Introduction," n. 1.

[21] (Ithaca, NY: Cornell University Press, 1990).

Jane Chance, the series editor; Caroline Palmer, editorial director at Boydell and Brewer; and the unnamed reader whose comments on a draft of this book were very helpful. For their time and attention as I attempted to locate Anne of France's manuscript and the sixteenth-century editions, I would also like to thank A. P. Romanov of the National Library of Russia; Marie-Elisabeth Boutroue of the Institut de Recherche et d'Histoire des Textes, Centre Nationale de la Recherche, France; and, especially, Nicolas Petit, Conservateur à la Réserve des livres rares, Bibliothèque nationale de France. Closer to home, I would not have been able to complete this project without the help of Sue Golden, Inter-Library Loan Coordinator of the Mortvedt Library. And I owe a special debt of thanks to my dear friend Tom Campbell and to my son, Kristian Jansen Jaech, both of whom probably heard more about Anne of France and her lessons than they wanted to, but who listened nevertheless.

Introduction

Anne of France, *Madame la Grande*

One of the most powerful women of the late fifteenth century, Anne of France is relatively unknown today, at least to those of us whose first language is English. While she is occasionally mentioned in the political biographies of her father, Louis XI of France, and her brother, Charles VIII, her own story remains unfamiliar, and the book of advice she composed for her daughter was last edited in the nineteenth century and has never before been translated into English.[1] Yet in the waning years of the fifteenth century, *Madame la Grande*, as she was known to her contemporaries, controlled the government of France for eight years, guiding it through a series of political crises that threatened the state from without and, perhaps more ominously, from within.

Born in 1461, Anne was the third child of Louis of France and his second wife, Charlotte of Savoy, but the first to survive more than a few months after birth.[2] Although we know where she was born—at

---

[1] The excellent multiple-biography by Pauline Matarasso is in part focused on Anne of France; see *Queen's Mate: Three Women of Power in France on the Eve of the Renaissance* (Burlington, VT: Ashgate Publishing, 2001), especially Part One (Chapters 1–7), 9–48; Chapter 18, 105–9; Chapter 29, 188–97; and Chapter 34, 233–44. See also my *The Monstrous Regiment of Women: Female Rulers in Early Modern Europe* (New York: Palgrave Macmillan, 2002), 54–64.

Anne is better known in France; recent biographies are Marc Chombart de Lauwe, *Anne de Beaujeu: ou la passion du pouvoir* (Paris: Librairie Jules Tallandier, 1980) and Pierre Pradel, *Anne de France, 1461–1522* (Paris: Editions Publisud, 1986), but both are lacking full documentation. Equally useful, despite its age, is Jehanne d'Orliac, *Anne de Beaujeu, roi de France* (Paris: Librairie Plon, 1926). In what follows, I rely on all three accounts, citing specific references when appropriate. All translations from these sources are my own. Henry Montaigu's *La Guerre des dames: La Fin des féodaux* (Paris: Olivier Orban, 1981) follows the lives of Anne of France; her sister Jeanne of France; Anne of Brittany, twice queen of France, married to Charles VIII and Louis XII; Louise of Savoy and Margaret of Austria, both of whom were raised by Anne of France; and Claude of France, Anne of Brittany's daughter.

[2] Louis was married first to Margaret of Scotland, who died in 1445. In exile for his rebellion against his father, Charles VII of France, Louis married Charlotte of Savoy (b. c. 1439) in 1458, without his father's permission. The first two

the chateau of Genappe, some thirty miles north of Brussels—we do not know exactly when, only that her birth preceded the death of her grandfather Charles VII on 22 July of that year. Only a few months after her father became king, he began the process of securing political alliances through her marriage. On 27 November 1461, Louis betrothed his only child to Nicholas, the grandson of René of Anjou; by the end of 1462, that alliance was abandoned in favor of an Aragonese match, that project, in turn, giving way to proposals for her marriage to Edward IV of England, then to Francis of Brittany, and even to the French king's own brother, Charles, duke of Berry.[3]

Meanwhile, we have very few details about Anne's childhood. On becoming king, Louis XI had installed his mother, his wife, and his infant daughter in the chateau of Amboise; there, the princess was attended by a *demoiselle d'honneur*, at least two chambermaids, several nurses, and a woman hired to rock her cradle.[4] This female household has not been kindly assessed by Anne's French biographers, who variously describe Amboise as a prison, an isolated fortress, or as a "royal gynecium"; we might instead regard it as a kind of "city of ladies," a remarkable environment that made possible the development of a remarkable woman.[5]

Just as little is known about Anne's life at Amboise, little has been written about her mother, Charlotte of Savoy, but that "little" is very negative. One contemporary noted that while she was "an excellent princess in other respects," she was "not a person in whom a man could take any great delight," another that she failed to inspire the king's

children born to the couple were Joachim (1459) and Louise (1460); both de Lauwe and Pradel include detailed genealogical tables.

3   Pradel, 13–19. René was the brother of Louis XI's mother, Marie of Anjou. Anne was only eight when her marriage to Edward IV (b. 1442) was proposed, prompting the Milanese ambassador to France to remark that the English king must be "very little" (15); Francis II of Brittany (b. 1435) was even older than Edward IV. Louis applied for a papal dispensation for his daughter's marriage to her uncle, but his plans were interrupted when his brother Charles died in 1472.

4   Pradel, 12. Charlotte of Savoy died in 1483, and her will lists members of her household, including Marie de Verdun, who had been Anne's nurse, and Guichon du Bois and Katherine de Brucelles, who had been Anne's chambermaids; see A. Tuetey, "Inventaire des biens de Charlotte de Savoy," *Bibliothèque de l'École de chartes* 26 (1865), 342–43.

5   For the assessments of the royal establishment at Amboise, see d'Orliac, 26; de Lauwe, 25; Pradel, 12. On the significance of such spaces for women's development, see Gerda Lerner, "Female Clusters, Female Networks, Social Spaces" in her *Women and History*, vol. 2: *The Creation of a Feminist Consciousness: From the Middle Ages to Eighteen-seventy* (New York: Oxford University Press, 1993), 220–46.

sexual desire.[6] Modern historians, at least the few who have mentioned her, have been no more kind, dismissing her as a charming but lifeless non-entity, as a sad, prematurely aged romantic, as a saint-like figure "crowned with a halo of sweetness and modesty" who knew nothing about politics, or as "feeble in health and weak in character."[7] But surely she was something more. As the daughter of Anne of Lusignan, Charlotte of Savoy was raised by a mother of considerable political influence and skill, while the contents of her personal library indicate the breadth of her intellectual interests.[8]

Louis XI's mother, Marie of Anjou, was also part of the Amboise household for the first years of Anne's life. The dowager queen was the daughter of the formidable Yolanda of Aragon, who for fifteen years ruled Anjou as its regent; while Marie may have been "delicate," as one modern biographer has described her, she is also credited with having been the source not only of her son's good sense but also for the "discreet work" of diplomacy that reconciled her husband and her brother.[9]

Whatever else happened in the chateau of Amboise during Anne's childhood, her biographer Jehanne d'Orliac seems rightly to have concluded that her intelligence was "ripened" there.[10] Meanwhile, her father may certainly have abhorred the "intrigues" and "coquetries" of women in general, and the person of his wife in particular, but he must also have recognized both the political expediencies of a female regent and the ability of women to succeed in such a role.[11] His paternal grandmother, Isabel of Bavaria, had been regent of France, and, as we have seen, his maternal grandmother had ruled Anjou for her son.

[6] Philippe de Commynes (1447–1511), whose *Mémoires* were translated by Andrew R. Scoble as *The Memoirs of Philip de Commines . . . Containing the Histories of Louis XI and Charles VIII . . .* (London: Henry G. Bohn, 1856), 2:80; Claude de Seyssel (c. 1450–1520), *Les Louenges du bon roy de France, Louis XII,* quoted by de Lauwe, 23 n. 2.

[7] d'Orliac, 30; de Lauwe, 24–5; Pradel, 35; and John S. C. Bridge, *A History of France from the Death of Louis XI,* vol. 1: *Reign of Charles VIII, Regency of Anne of Beaujeu, 1483–1493* (1921; rpt. New York: Octagon Books, 1978), 27.

[8] Anne of Lusignan (c. 1420s–1460s) married Louis of Savoy; after 1439, he left governing responsibilities to her (see Jansen, 245 n. 149). The contents of Charlotte of Savoy's library are included in Tuetey's inventory; see below, 11.

[9] For Marie of Anjou (c. 1410–1463), see Jansen, 37; for the assessments of her role, see Pradel, 13. For Yolanda of Aragon (1380–c. 1430), wife of Louis II of Anjou and regent of Anjou for her son Louis III, see Jansen, 241 n. 100.

[10] d'Orliac, 33.

[11] d'Orliac, 30. On the "genesis" of the regency as a political "vocation" for women in France, see André Poulet, "Capetian Women and the Regency: The Genesis of a Vocation," in John Carmi Parsons, ed., *Medieval Queenship* (New York: St. Martin's Press, 1993), 93–116 and Jansen, 57–60 and 247–49.

One sister, Yolande of Valois, was regent of Savoy for her son, Philibert, another, Madeleine, was regent of Foix for her daughter, Catherine, who inherited the throne of Navarre as queen regnant; in England, the king's cousin Margaret of Anjou played an active role in the battle to preserve the throne of England for her son, Edward.[12] Whatever he felt about his queen, Louis left his son, the *dauphin* Charles, in the female universe of Amboise, while his daughter Anne became part of his court at Plessis-les-Tours; after her marriage to Pierre of Beaujeu in November of 1473, Anne seems to have spent much of the next ten years in the company of her father.[13] "She is the least foolish of women," he is famously to have said, "—and as for wise women, there are none."[14]

When Louis XI died in 1483, his son and heir Charles was thirteen years old, arguably old enough to succeed to the French throne in his own right, but the aging king circumvented the argument. Just before his death, Louis transferred custody of his son to his daughter and her husband. His son-in-law was a loyal and firm presence, but lacked political skill or insight; Louis named Pierre of Beaujeu lieutenant-general of France.[15] The twenty-two-year-old Anne, on the other hand, was different. To this "least foolish of women," he entrusted the *dauphin*'s care and education, leaving to her the responsibility to govern France, if not the title of regent.[16] Lacking

---

[12]   Isabel of Bavaria (1371–1435) was regent of France during Charles VI's periods of insanity. Yolande of Valois (1434–78) married Amadeus IX of Savoy. Madeleine of Valois (1440–80) married Gaston of Foix, her daughter Catherine (1468–1517) inheriting the throne of Navarre in her own right; interestingly, Anne of France played a role in ensuring Catherine's succession (Bridge, 4:174). Margaret of Anjou (1430–82), the daughter of René of Anjou and Isabelle of Lorraine, married Henry VI of England. She is best known to English speakers today as the mad prophetess in Shakespeare's *Richard III*, but see the new biography by Helen E. Maurer, *Margaret of Anjou: Queenship and Power in Late Medieval England* (Woodbridge: The Boydell Press, 2003).

[13]   See d'Orliac, 35–37 and Paul Pélicier, *Essai sur le gouvernement de la Dame de Beaujeu, 1483–1491* (Chartres: Imprimerie Édouard Garnier, 1882), 45–6. Anne was born before July of 1461, so she was about twelve-and-a-half years old at the time of her marriage to Pierre of Beaujeu (b. 1438). The *dauphin* Charles was born in 1471. (A second daughter, Jeanne, had been born to the royal couple in 1464; shortly after her birth she was sent to Lignières and raised there. The king did not see her again until her marriage in 1476.)

[14]   Quoted in Jean-Marie de la Mure, *Histoire des ducs de Bourbon et des comtes de Forez . . .* , ed. R. Chantelauze (Paris: A. Montbrison, 1868), 2:326 n.

[15]   For the reports of a number of contemporary chroniclers, see de la Mure, 2:325–27 nn.

[16]   On Louis XI's arrangements for his son's guardianship, see "Appendix I," 91.

the name of regent, Anne of France was nevertheless recognized as controlling the person of the king, the finances of the state, and the power of the realm.[17] In his account of her role during the period from 1483 to 1491, historian John Bridge concludes, "We can affirm . . . that the lady of Beaujeu really governed France during the first years of the nominal reign of her brother."[18]

When Anne of France left the court in 1491, she was thirty years old, but rather than retiring, she was, instead, beginning a new phase of her political career. In the years following her marriage, she and her husband had been rewarded and enriched first by her father and then by her brother; when the duke of Bourbon, Pierre of Beaujeu's oldest brother, died without an heir, she acted quickly and ruthlessly. In securing the title for her husband, she "gave herself alone the duchy of the Bourbons."[19] In gaining Bourbon, she secured independence for herself, and for her daughter, Suzanne, who was born on 10 May 1491. In her chateau of Chantelle, not far from the Bourbon capital of Moulins, Anne reigned as sovereign, signing acts with the royal formula *Car tel est notre plaisir* ("for such is our pleasure") and reorganizing and codifying the laws of the Bourbonnais.[20] She also recreated the "city of ladies" of her childhood at Amboise, educating and training a generation of young girls as they grew into women. As the inveterate gossip Pierre de Brantôme noted, "there

---

[17] The most accessible account of the period is Bridge, vol. 1: *Reign of Charles VIII, Regency of Anne of Beaujeu, 1483–1493*; as an indication of her accomplishments, here is a brief extract from the heading "Anne of Beaujeu" in his index: "establishes her influence . . . ; convenes the States-General . . . ; approached by the Breton rebels . . . ; temporizes with the Breton rebels . . . ; crushes an Orleanist plot . . . ; gains support . . . ; [enters into] treaties with Flemish towns and Breton rebels . . . ; defeats an Austrian plot in Burgundy . . . ; defeats the feudal coalition . . . ; [goes to] war with Maximilian [of Austria] . . . ; . . . subdues Guyenne . . . ; . . . plays on Breton jealousies . . . ; [accepts] surrender of Nantes . . . ; [undertakes] negotiations with England . . . ; [arranges] marriage of Charles VIII. . . ." Bridge's history is based almost entirely on contemporary sources (see his bibliography, 262–78). See also Pélicier.

[18] Bridge, 1:49, confirming the judgment of Pélicier, viii.

[19] d'Orliac, 98.

[20] For the assessment of her role as "sovereign" of Bourbon and the royal formula, see d'Orliac, 119 and de Lauwe, 386–87 and 417–19. Matarasso agrees that "in the Borbonnais [Anne of France] was also queen in her own right" (106). On Charles VIII's granting of "royal rights" to the Beaujeus and Anne's *grande oeuvre* in reorganizing the Customary of Bourbonnais, see de la Mure, 2:438 n and 455 n.

were no ladies or daughters of great houses in her time who did not receive lessons from her, the house of Bourbon being one of the greatest and most splendid in Christendom"; on this point he had good authority, since his grandmother Louise de Daillon was among those daughters who had been brought up by Anne of France.[21]

And she also remained involved in affairs of state. When her brother invaded Italy in 1494, he arranged for his sister, not his wife, to manage in his absence, and like his father, in making this unorthodox arrangement he avoided the official designation of regent; instead, by the "express order of the king," his queen, Anne of Brittany, was placed in his sister's guardianship, and the government of France was "transported" to her court at Moulins.[22] One of her contemporaries, the king's secretary André de la Vigne, offered his assessment of her role in a poem composed in her honor: "lady without peer" and "great duchess," he wrote, she ensured the safety of France during the king's absence in Italy, earning the gratitude and the praise of all.[23]

By the time the king returned from Italy in 1495, his son, the French *dauphin*, was dead; three years later, Charles VIII of France, not quite twenty-eight years old, was also dead. The new king was

---

[21] Pierre de Bourdeille, abbé of Brantôme (c. 1540–1614), spent his childhood at the court of Marguerite of Angoulême (1492–1549), queen consort of Henry II of Navarre. The 1535 edition of Anne's *enseignements* was dedicated to Marguerite, the daughter of Louise of Savoy and the sister of Francis of Angoulême, who would become king of France as Francis I. Brantôme's mother and grandmother were both members of Marguerite's Navarrese court. According to Brantôme, his portrait of Anne is drawn from many of her letters, written to members of his family, though most of her letters, including those claimed by Brantôme, are now lost; his *Vies des dames illustres* was published posthumously. I have used the translation by Katharine Prescott Wormeley, *Illustrious Dames of the Court of Valois Kings* (New York: Lamb Publishing, 1912); the biographical portrait of Anne of France is found on pp. 216–18, the quotation from p. 218.

[22] d'Orliac, 123–24 and Pradel, 121–24. Pradel notes that Pierre of Beaujeu, now duke of Bourbon, was given his old title of "lieutenant general," but adds that "to name him" was also "to name Madam" (130). About the Bourbon collaboration, Matarasso comments, "Madame may have had no official status, but in the king's absence and her own palace it was impossible she should be anywhere but at the centre. . . . Indeed it was debatable who, during the next fifteen months, was the true queen of France . . ." (92). On the Italian campaign of Charles VIII of France, see Bridge, vol. 2.

The chateau of Moulins is now a museum named in honor of Anne of France, Musée Anne de Beaujeu. The chateau and museum can be viewed on-line; see http://www.musee-moulins.fr.

[23] The *rondeau* de la Vigne composed in praise of Anne of France is quoted in de la Mure, 2:443 n.

Louis XII, whose rebellion in the first years of Charles VIII's reign had culminated in the aptly named "Mad War."[24] At least one observer thought that Anne of France might intervene in the succession—it was reported that "she thought for a moment to claim the crown for herself, saying that 'she was the first among the descendants of the kings of France.' "[25] Although she had no such intention, the new king decided "to call his old adversary to his aid"; in exchange for her support, he awarded her more land, more titles, more revenue and, more important, the assurance that her daughter Suzanne would inherit Bourbon after Pierre's death.[26]

Although Anne of France would also survive Louis XII, we will end our discussion of her life here, for the moment. It is important to note, however, that she never withdrew entirely from the political center of government; she regularly attended affairs of state, like Louis XII's entry into Paris, to name only one example, and in 1503, when he fell ill, it appeared as if the king might call upon her to take control of the government of France once more.[27] Although he survived this illness, when his death was imminent in 1514, he designated Anne of France

---

[24] When Charles VIII became king of France, Louis of Orléans became heir-presumptive to the throne and expected that he would be regent of France. When the Estates-General of France decided against him, he attempted a civil rising and demanded that the parliament of Paris support his claims—but, like the Estates, the parliament decided against him. Louis then retreated to Nantes; he gained the support of Francis II, duke of Brittany, signed an accord with England guaranteeing its support, and negotiated an alliance with Maximilian of Austria. The result was the Mad War, which began in 1485; it eventually became a European conflict, pitting Louis and his allies—Brittany, Austria, England, and Spain— against Anne, who occupied Orléans, incited the Flemish against Maximilian, and turned one of Louis' chief supporters, Alain d'Albret, duke of Guyenne, against him. Louis of Orléans was taken captive on 28 July 1488, but his allies fought on until the death of the duke of Brittany in 1489. For a complete discussion of the Mad War, see Bridge, 1:132–219.

[25] Anne's words are reported in a seventeenth-century history; see de Lauwe, 357 n.

[26] Charles VIII died on 7 April 1498; Pierre of Bourbon paid homage to Louis XII as the new king the next day (de Lauwe, 357 n). For the new king's awards to Anne of France and Pierre of Bourbon, see d'Orliac, 139–47; de Lauwe, 357–76; Pradel, 161–73. For a summary of what Anne of France's support cost Louis XII, see Matarasso, 146–48. The collaboration of the one-time adversaries was so solid that d'Orliac claims that before his invasion of Italy, Louis XII designated Anne of France as "regent" in his absence, 161.

[27] d'Orliac, 165–68 and Pradel, 178. A couple of years earlier, in 1501, Pierre de Rohan, Marshall de Gié, had suggested Anne was planning to marry Suzanne to Francis, the heir presumptive, and set herself up once more as regent of France; see Matarasso, 203.

to take charge of any posthumously born prince.[28] She was in Paris in 1515 when Louis XII died, and it was again said that she would take control of the government herself.[29] But that was just a rumor; she was in Reims for the coronation of Francis I and in Paris to witness his entry into the city. She herself would live until 1522, her life spanning the reigns of four French kings.

Lessons for My Daughter: sources and models

We do not know when Anne of France composed her lessons for Suzanne. In his introduction to her text, Chazaud asserts that the work was written between the death of Pierre of Bourbon on 10 October 1503 and Suzanne's marriage to her cousin Charles Montpensier, 10 May 1505. The only evidence he provides for this claim is the comment that when Suzanne married she was "just at the point of entering her fifteenth year," that her education was finished, and that, as a "far-sighted" mother, Anne wanted to ensure her daughter received "the treasure of her experience."[30]

Chazaud may be correct in this date. Certainly Anne makes no reference to Pierre of Bourbon in her lessons, and she writes about Suzanne's marriage as something that is yet to take place. But, just as certainly, she writes as if the question of Suzanne's marriage were undecided; she counsels her daughter about how to behave if she finds herself married to a foreign prince and living far from all that was familiar, where even clothing and customs were different. As early as 1493, Charles VIII had considered a match that would unite his niece with one of the Sforzas of Milan, a possibility that Anne resisted, saying that the last thing she wanted for her daughter was a marriage in Lombardy, where wives were treated badly.[31] The king had also considered an alliance with Maximilian of Austria; for a time it seemed as if Suzanne would marry Philip of Burgundy, the emperor's son and heir, and become empress of the Holy Roman empire some day.[32] In 1495 Charles had proposed a Neapolitan

---

[28] Pradel, 197. Louis XII had recently married Mary Tudor, his third wife, hoping for a male heir.

[29] For this rumor, see Matarasso, 286.

[30] Chazaud, xxxii. Suzanne was born on 10 May 1491. Chazaud's dating of the composition of the *enseignements* has been accepted by the relatively few who have examined Anne's *enseignements*, from Alice A. Hentsch, *De la Littérature didactique du moyenâge, s'adressant spécialement aux femmes* (Cahors, France: A. Coueslant, 1903), 199 to Matarasso, 191.

[31] Anne of France is quoted by Pradel, 121.

[32] Pradel, 125–27.

marriage for Suzanne, and in January 1497 he was again considering the possibility of a marriage between Suzanne and Ludovico Sforza's son.[33] But well before the period Chazaud suggests for the composition of the *Lessons*, it had been decided that Suzanne's marriage would not ally her to a foreign prince after all; she would be married within France, either to the young duke of Alençon or to a member of the cadet branch of the Bourbon family.[34]

In the meantime, Anne of France suffered a mysterious illness late in 1497, one that kept her in Moulins even when her brother died in April of 1498. Her biographer Pierre Pradel argues that the reason for the "agitation" in the court of Moulins—and the cause of her illness—was a late pregnancy and the death of the baby, a boy.[35] Whether or not Anne's "anguish" was the result of a stillborn child, the circumstances of her life in 1497 and 1498 suggest to me a much more likely date for the composition of the *Lessons*. During this period, Anne of France was only in her mid-thirties, but suffering from some kind of serious illness, one that might well have caused her to reflect on her own mortality—as her text begins, in fact, she alludes to her expectations of an "imminent, sudden, and early death," and her fears may reflect more than literary formula or fiction. Her brother Charles had just died at age twenty-eight; her husband, at age sixty, could not be expected to live for too many more years. This period of death and change and uncertainty may well have motivated her to address her daughter in writing; throughout her lessons she constantly reminds Suzanne of the transience of life and the mutability of fortune. And many of Anne's instructions—avoid making faces, refrain from running or jumping, say your prayers every morning, pay attention in church, keep your fingers out of your nose, dress warmly when the weather is cold—make far more sense if they are addressed to a child of seven or eight than they do if they are intended for Suzanne on the eve of her marriage. By our standards, Suzanne of Bourbon was still a child when she was married at age fourteen, but by the standards of

---

[33] Pradel, 135, 152–53.

[34] Pradel, 175–80. Louis XII favored a marriage between Suzanne and Charles of Alençon, son of one of his supporters, a proposal Pierre of Bourbon preferred; Anne's favorite candidate was Charles of Montpensier, who eventually became Suzanne's husband.

[35] Pradel, 155–56. Anne had given birth to a son, named Charles, in 1476; the baby died while in infancy (see de la Mure, 2:307 n and 411 n). Matarasso notes the oddity of Anne's role after Charles VIII's death, commenting that she "chose for once to leave the negotiations to her husband," 146; Pradel's theory makes sense of Anne of France's behavior at this critical time.

her time and class—Anne of France had been married at age twelve—Suzanne was surely past the need for such basic instruction. I would argue that her lessons were composed during the uncertainties of 1497 and 1498 rather than six or seven years later.[36]

Throughout her work, Anne of France refers to a wide range of authorities, both classical and Christian; she cites Socrates, Aristotle, Cato, Ovid, and Boethius, on the one hand, and Ambrose, Augustine, John Chrysostom, Bernard of Clairvaux, Thomas Aquinas, and Leonard of Udine, on the other. She quotes the Bible, though not very often; a stoic view of life pervades her work. She also compiles a reading list for Suzanne, not only recommending specific books as a way to occupy the time but insisting that such study is way to self-improvement.[37] Even so, we might be tempted to dismiss all her references as generalities, or as her demonstration of her familiarity with famous men and their learned books but for one crucial point—we know that Anne of France owned numerous works by the authorities she cites and that she owned copies of all of the books on her reading list.

We are particularly fortunate to have two library inventories, one of the Bourbon library at Aigueperse, compiled in 1507 on Anne of France's orders, the second of the library at Moulins, completed in September 1523, ten months after her death. The Bourbon library lists some 170 volumes, and categorizes the holdings by language, including those written in French, Latin, Italian, English, Flemish, and Spanish. The library at Moulins was nearly twice as large; the inventory catalogues 324 items, many of them multi-volume works or anthologies.[38] Every author or text Anne cites or recommends in

---

36   The period between Pierre of Bourbon's death (1503) and Suzanne's marriage to Charles Montpensier (1505) seems, by contrast, to be filled with much less uncertainty than this earlier period—Louis XII had been king for five years, Pierre of Bourbon's death could not have been too surprising, and Anne of France was free to arrange her daughter's marriage as she wished.

37   For this reading list, see *Lessons*, Section IV.

38   Chazaud prints these inventories, 213–58. There is no information about the libraries of other Bourbon possessions, especially of the library at Chantelle, Anne's favorite and long-time residence. The number of volumes in each library is only an estimate, since those who compiled the inventories sometimes counted each volume of a two-volume work as separate items, and sometimes counted multi-volume works as a single item. At Moulins, for example, the first and second volumes of *la vie nostre Seigneur* are numbered as items 21 and 22, while "*cinq volumes de la Fleur des histories*" is counted as a single entry, item 29. Items 310–14 comprise a five-volume set of anthologies of the works of Christine de Pizan, the matching volumes bound in red velvet and closed with jeweled clasps.

her lessons appears in these two library inventories. Even more interesting, we can trace many of the books in the Moulins library back
to Anne of France's mother, Charlotte of Savoy.

As we have seen, Charlotte of Savoy has been ignored or dismissed
by historians and biographers. Her influence on her son Charles VIII
has been viewed negatively; as Pauline Matarasso indicates, historians
have "blamed Charles VIII's vainglorious dreams on his mother's
fondness for reading romances of chivalry."[39] Among the inventory
of her personal possessions made at the time of her death—clothing,
jewels, tapestries, furniture—were some 138 books; a few of them, to
be sure, were romances, but her library also included psalters, books
of hours, saints' lives, and other devotional works, as well as numerous histories and books on good government.[40] She owned the work
of a few classical authors (Cicero, for example), translations of
Boethius' *Consolation of Philosophy*, works by Boccaccio, a book on
herbs and trees, a collection of medical recipes, and a number of books
by Christine de Pizan, including *The Treasure of the City of Ladies*,
often suggested as a model for Anne of France's lessons. While
Charlotte of Savoy's contribution to her daughter's development has
been judged negligible, her library must have been a part of Anne's
childhood at Amboise, its many books a considerable part of her education. In fact, all of the books Anne includes in her specific reading
list for Suzanne are books that Charlotte of Savoy owned, books that
must have been part of her daughter's education, books that Anne of
France inherited when her mother died in 1483, and books that were
in the Moulins library at the time of her own death in 1522.[41]

---

[39] Matarasso, 17.
[40] The number of "books" is my own count, based on Tuetey's publication of the
inventory, but it's hard to tell whether some of the books, described in the inventory as in bad (*méchant*) condition, worn (*tout derrompu*), or worth nothing,
should be counted; one "item" in the inventory is comprised of seven notebooks
or sheets, another is described as a "little book" containing only a page and a half
of writing. Among the books on government are *ung livre de l'Instruction d'un
jeune prince* (359) and *le livre du Gouvernement des roys et princes* (360), which
Tuetey believes to be a translation of *De Regimene principum* by Gilles de Rome.
[41] In printing the inventory of the Moulins library, Chazaud marked out some
35 books that had come to Anne from her mother's library. But in laying the detailed
inventories side by side and using the same descriptions Chazaud did, I count at
least 67 volumes in Moulins that came from Charlotte of Savoy—in other words,
about half of the books her mother owned. Did the other half of Charlotte of Savoy's
library go to her second daughter, Jeanne of France? If so, perhaps they ultimately
came to Anne of France since we know that when Jeanne died in 1505, Anne and
Suzanne inherited her personal possessions (Pradel, 185; see also René de Maulde

Thus when Anne of France decided to write a series of instructions for her daughter, she had not only the education that would enable her undertake the task but a room of her own and a library at hand that she could draw upon while she wrote. Books were important to her, and we know that she saw them as more than a way of passing time. As she tells us, they provide models for living, and just one instance of the value she saw in books is cited by Matarasso: "The carefully chosen gift Madame brought back for [her brother] when she made her dash in April 1488 to secure the Bourbonnais was a copy of Joinville's *Histoire de Saint Louis*, taken from the ducal library." Charles VIII did, indeed, emulate the model this book provided; as Matarasso notes, ". . . Charles can be seen deliberately patterning his life and actions on those of his forebear."[42]

As for Anne herself, models for her composition were also to be found in the books she possessed. The relatively few scholars who have written about her lessons have generally cited three of particular importance for her, *Le Livre du chevalier de la Tour Landry pour l'enseignement de ses filles*, *Le Ménagier de Paris*, and Christine de Pizan's *Le Livre des tois vertus*, or, to give them their more common English titles, *The Book of the Knight of the Tower*, *The Goodman of Paris*, and *The Treasure of the City of Ladies*.[43] All three are conduct

la Clavière, *Jeanne de France, duchesse d'Orléans et de Berry [1464–1505]* [Paris: H. Champion, 1883], 461–67). It should also be noted that Anne of France inherited her aunt Jeanne of France's possessions as well, including a number of books; the elder Jeanne of France (d. 1482), was not only Anne's aunt but her sister-in-law, married to Jean II of Bourbon, Pierre of Bourbon's brother. Patricia Thompson indicates that Anne of France's library eventually became part of the Saint-Germain collection and, ultimately, was acquired by Dubrovski; see her "Biography of a Library: The Western European Manuscript Collection of Peter P. Dubrovskii in Leningrad," *The Journal of Library History* 9 (1984), 482.

42 Matarasso, 124.
43 *Le Livre du chevalier de la Tour Landry pour l'enseignement de ses filles*, ed. M. Anatole de Montaiglon (Paris: P. Jannet, 1854), translated into English and published by William Caxton as *The Book of the Knight of the Tower*, ed. M. Y. Offord (London: Oxford University Press, 1971); *Le Ménagier de Paris*, ed. Georgine E. Brereton and Janet M. Ferrier (London: Oxford University Press, 1981), translated into English and abridged by Tanya Bayard, *A Medieval Home Companion: Housekeeping in the Fourteenth Century* (New York: HarperCollins, 1991); and *Le Livre des trois vertus*, ed. Charity Cannon Willard and Eric Hicks (Paris: Librairie Honoré Champion, 1989), translated into English by Sarah Lawson, *Christine de Pisan: The Treasure of the City of Ladies, or the Book of the Three Virtues* (New York: Penguin Books, 1985).
    Specific studies of Anne of France's lessons are limited to Joseph Viple, *Les Enseignements d'Anne de France* (Moulins: Crépin-Leblond, 1935); Charity Cannon Willard, "Anne de France, Reader of Christine de Pizan" in Glenda

books, that is, books intended to provide their female readers with rules for living and models of appropriate behavior.[44] All three were composed about a hundred years before Anne of France sat down to write, Geoffroy de la Tour Landry composing his *enseignements* between 1371 and 1372, the unnamed bourgeois "goodman" writing his guide to household management for his fifteen-year-old bride around the year 1393, and Christine de Pizan completing her "treasure" for women about 1405.[45] Anne of France owned or had access to all three books; the inventory of the library at Moulins lists two copies of the knight's book for his daughters, one of which had come

K. McLeod, ed., *The Reception of Christine de Pizan from the Fifteenth through the Nineteenth Centuries: Visitors to the City* (Lewiston, NY: Edwin Mellen Press, 1991), 59–70; and Roberta L. Krueger, "*Chascune selon son estat*: Women's Education and Social Class in the Conduct Books of Christine de Pizan and Anne de France," *Papers on French Seventeenth Century Literature* 24.46 (1997), 19–34. Relatively little of Viple's work is analysis—rather, he translates some sections of Anne's *enseignements* into modern French, but most of his book consists of huge chunks Anne's original French, quoted from Chazaud's original (and not quoted altogether accurately). Neither Willard nor Krueger go beyond generalities in dealing with Anne's text. Much more detailed are Hentsch, 199–207 and Matarasso, 12–13, 38, 107, 191–94.

One additional precedent for Anne's text, now lost, should be noted here. Hentsch indicates that Elizabeth of Bosnia (c. 1339–1385) wrote a *Manuel d'éducation pour ses filles*, but it no longer survives. It was known in France; a copy was sent in 1374 to Louis de France, count of Valois (135). Elizabeth of Bosnia was the wife of Louis of Anjou, king of Hungary and Poland. Their older daughter Maria (1365–c. 1394) became queen of Hungary, their younger daughter, Jadwiga (1372–1399), queen of Poland.

[44] On conduct books for women, see Hentsch, cited above, n. 30; Diane Bornstein, *The Lady in the Tower: Medieval Courtesy Literature for Women* (Hamden: Archon Books, 1983); Colette H. Winn, " '*De mères en filles*': Les manuels d'éducation sous l'Ancien Régime," *Atlantis* 19.1 (1983), 23–29; Colette H. Winn, "La *Dignitas Mulieris*: Les Enjeux idéologiques d'une appropriation du xvᵉ au xviiᵉ siècle," *Études Littéraires* 27.2 (1994), 11–24; Felicity Riddy, "Mother Knows Best: Reading Social Change in a Courtesy Text," *Speculum* 71.1 (1996), 66–86; and Susan Udry, "Books of Women's Conduct from France during the High and Late Middle Ages, 1200–1400," ORB Online Encyclopedia; available from http://the-orb.net/encyclop/culture/women/books4women.htm; accessed 9 May 2003. Anne's text is mentioned by Bornstein, 71–72, 74; Winn, "Les manuels d'éducation," 23, 25, 26–27; and "Les enjeux idéologiques,"12, 15 n. 15, 16.

[45] In his prologue, Geoffroy writes that he began his composition in 1371, and two references in his text indicate he is still at work in 1372 (his daughters are Jeanne, Anne, and Marie). In his prologue, the unnamed Paris husband says he is writing because his new bride of fifteen has asked for instruction. Christine de Pizan dedicated her book to Margaret of Burgundy (m. 31 August 1404), the eleven-year-old bride of Louis de Guyenne.

from her mother's library, and multiple copies of Christine's "treasure," two of which came from her mother. The Bourbon library at Aigueperse had a copy of the Goodman's book.

All three instruct women in appropriate behavior: how to love and worship God, how to conduct themselves prudently and virtuously while avoiding gossip, idleness, and envy, how to honor their parents, how to obey their husbands and manage their households, how to avoid extravagance in dress that might damage their husbands' reputation, and how to raise dutiful children. These are concerns that Anne addresses too, as we shall see, but any similarities seem more the result of their shared ideals of female behavior than Anne's deliberate use of these texts as models. Significantly, she neither alludes to them nor recommends them to Suzanne. I would argue that, rather than finding a model in conduct books for women, Anne of France looked instead to her forebears, the Valois kings.

The renowned Louis IX wrote two sets of *enseignements*, one for his son Philip, who succeeded his father as king, and another for his daughter Isabelle, who became queen of Navarre.[46] Indeed Anne seems to direct her daughter's attention specifically to the precepts of Louis IX, canonized in 1297; the first item on her reading list for Suzanne is the "small book" of "the noble Saint Louis."[47] To Philip, the king recommended loving God, meeting adversity with patience, paying attention in church, praying to God with both his heart and his lips, relieving a burdened heart to his confessor, and honoring his father and mother, all advice that Anne, in turn, gives her daughter. In terms of Philip's duty as king, his father advised him to surround himself with "worthy men" and "eschew the company of the wicked" and to uphold the good customs of the realm. Philip should see that his subjects "live under [him] in peace and uprightness"; he should "maintain the good cities and commons of [his] realm" and "beware of undertaking a war against any Christian prince without good deliberation." To his "dear daughter," Louis IX recommended praying to God with "all her heart and all her power," making frequent

---

[46] Louis IX (1214–70) was the son of Blanche of Castile, who had ruled France as regent for him during his minority. His son Philip "the Bold" (1245–85) succeeded him as king of France. His daughter Isabelle of Valois (1241–71) married Thibaut II of Navarre.

[47] For his *enseignements* for Philip, see David O'Connell, *The Teachings of Saint Louis: A Critical Text* (Chapel Hill, NC: The University of North Carolina Press, 1972); Chazaud prints the instructions for Isabelle, xx–xxvii. The quotations from both are my own translation.

Anne's reading list for Suzanne is found in her *Lessons*, Section IV.

confession, taking pleasure in speaking about God, suffering illness patiently, taking pity on the suffering of others, keeping the secrets of others, obeying her husband humbly, avoiding extravagant clothing, or, in other words, "taking great care to be so perfect that those who hear about you or see you will find in you a good example." This advice, too, is passed on to Suzanne. These two sets of lessons are fairly general, and yet in their conception, organization, and presentation, they seem far more likely to have provided Anne a model for her *enseignements* than the conduct books written for women.[48] Most strikingly, they offer Anne a convention that allows her to do what is utterly unconventional—under the guise of a parent offering advice to a princess, she can also incorporate advice appropriate for a prince.[49]

Anne could also look to her own father for a similarly ambiguous model. Just before his death in 1483, Louis XI ordered his astrologer and physician Pierre Choisnet to compile a kind of conduct book, known as *The Rosetree of Wars*, for his son. The book was intended to distill the king's experience in order to profit his son; as Louis noted in his prologue, the study of "past things is very profitable" not only as a comfort and consolation in times of adversity but also as a way of avoiding adversity in the first place.[50] As a way of conveying his wisdom, he employed the metaphor of the garden: "The king must think about the condition of his people, and he must visit them

---

[48] Matarasso (rightly, I believe) discounts Christine de Pisan's influence: "Christine de Pisan is often advanced as a formative influence. . . . I can find no supporting evidence in the *Enseignements*" (194 n. 18).

     In his discussion of the sources of Louis IX's instructions for his son, O'Connell notes the influence of his mother, Blanche of Castile, a "mighty force" in the development of his political thinking (52–53).

[49] The extent to which these three sets of *enseignements* can also be read as part of the medieval epistolary tradition remains to be investigated; for this insight, I am indebted to Jane Chance, series editor, Boydell and Brewer's Library of Medieval Women. In this sense, Anne of France's lessons for her daughter might be compared to verse epistles composed by Radegund of Poitiers (a life of the sixth-century saint, originally belonging to Charlotte of Savoy, was in the Moulins library); to the handbook composed by Dhuoda of Uzès for her son William; and to the letters of Catherine of Siena and Christine de Pizan; for an introduction to this genre and women writers in the Middle Ages, see Karen Cherewatuk and Ulrike Wiethaus, eds., *Dear Sister: Medieval Women and the Epistolary Genre* (Philadelphia: University of Pennsylvania Press, 1993).

[50] *Louis XI: Les Rozier des guerres*, ed. F. Leclerq (Paris: L'Insomniaque, 1994), 3–4. This is a facsimile of an edition printed in 1616, dedicated to the son of Henry IV. The quotations are my own translation.

often, as a good gardener does his garden."[51] The role of kings and princes, as Louis defined it, is "to defend the common good . . . and to uphold justice and peace among their subjects," doing what is good "in this world and in the other"; behaving otherwise and "doing evil" would only result in grief, and, in the end, "one must count one day on leaving this world to go and give an account of one's under-takings and receive one's reward."[52] After a lengthy discussion of justice, he turned his attention to the subject of war and warfare. If on his succession a prince finds his new kingdom peaceful, "he should be very happy and thank God and make sure he does not begin a war," for war brings "a great deal of peril, pain, tribulation, suffering, and destruction of people, land, and goods."[53] "In war there is no pleasure and never any profit," he warned, adding that "the only end of war was peace."[54] Despite his stated aversion to war, however, the king devoted the remainder of his instructions—five of the book's nine chapters—to advice about war and warfare.

Conscious always of her royal heritage, having served as virtual king of France for eight years, and in a moment when she faced her own mortality, Anne of France looked to her royal forebears when she decided to set down her own life-lessons for her daughter. Although clearly informed by her reading of books like those of Christine de Pizan—who was, like Anne herself, a woman writing to women—Anne aimed for something more than a simple guide to good behav-ior when she distilled her experience into the lessons she intended for her daughter. It is not coincidental that, in the list of instruction presented to her daughter, she presented her *enseignements* in thirty-three sections, the very same number Louis IX had composed for his son.[55] Nor does it seem coincidental that her book of advice was published in 1521, the year the first printed edition of her father's book appeared.[56]

---

[51] *Rozier*, 18–19.

[52] *Rozier*, 12–13.

[53] *Rozier*, 47.

[54] *Rozier*, 48, 60.

[55] While noting that there are "short," "long," and "interpolated" versions of Louis IX's instructions, O'Connell argues persuasively that the long version, thirty-three sections, is the "authentic" text. See *The Teachings of Saint Louis*, 20–45; his critical edition of the text is on pp. 55–60.

[56] Leclercq notes that the first edition of Louis XI's text, composed in 1483, was printed in Paris in 1521; "subsequent editions appeared in 1522, 1533, and 1616; a 1689 biography of Louis XI, which included the text of *The Rosetree of Wars*, was written for the education of Louis XIV (97–99).

Lessons for My Daughter: content and structure

Doubtless aware of the challenges posed by her task, Anne of France begins by subtly justifying her composition: her work originates in the "perfect natural love" of a mother for a daughter. Even while recognizing the wretchedness of human life in general, and her own "poor, rude, and limited ability" in particular, she nevertheless claims the authority, as a mother, to prepare "a few little lessons" for Suzanne. In committing an "unnatural" act, she thus presents her task as not just natural but perfectly natural, and after this initial gesture, her text bears none of the "anxieties of authorship" we characteristically see in texts authored by medieval women.[57]

Though Anne describes her instructions as "a few little lessons," begun without a "long introduction" and presented "in few words," her work belies this claim. This is a substantial work—some 14,000 words in translation—and a comprehensive one.[58] Just as her father had defined the ideal king, Anne used her lessons to construct an ideal princess. The formal introduction, one extended sentence with its grammatically paralleled components, is mirrored by an equally formal, though almost perfunctory, conclusion. The intervening lessons vary in length. Some of them are very short, like sections VII and XIII, for example, each of which is fewer than 200 words long. Others are much more substantial, running well over 1,000 words, with section XIX over 1,500 words.[59] In order to gauge the scope of Anne's ambitious task, we can contrast her lessons to those of

---

[57] For an excellent discussion of the "ideology of gender in the Middle Ages" and female authorship, see another volume in the Library of Medieval Women series, Dayle Seidenspinner-Núñez's *The Writings of Teresa de Cartegena* (Cambridge: D. S. Brewer, 1998), esp. 16–21; the critical essay is also relevant, particularly the section "From Anxiety of Authorship to *Admiraçion*: Autobiography, Authorship, and Authorization in the Works of Teresa de Cartagena," 113–17.

[58] In his edition of the text, Chazaud presents the *enseignements* in 31 divisions, each marked out with a roman numeral, but the sixteenth-century printed edition clearly marks out 33 sections with large capital letters. Chazaud indicates that there are no significant differences between the manuscript he saw in St. Petersburg and the first printed edition, an incomplete example of which he saw just as he was finishing his edition (x–xi). In comparing the two, he noted only a few textual variations (listed xii–xiv). The discrepancy between his divisions and the divisions in the sixteenth-century edition is, I think, the result of the incomplete state of the printed book he saw, compounded by his own error (see *Lessons*, n. 75).

[59] Despite the problems with his miscalculations, I have maintained Chazaud's section numbers here so that those who wish to compare this English translation with the original French will find the process easier.

Louis IX: among the thirty-three precepts he presented his son, several are under 25 words (number 12 is under 10 words), while the longest (number 24) is a little more than 200 words long.[60]

At first glance, there seems to be little organization in the *Lessons* beyond this division into sections, and even at second glance the text does not present us with a well-ordered, clearly structured composition. As Anne compiles her list, she seems to move from one topic to another as they suggest themselves to her; "and," "also," and "and also" introduce section after section, sentence after sentence. Her prose seems almost self-propelled as she strings phrases, clauses and sentences together with "and" and "because." She repeats herself. She returns to points she has made previously to reiterate them or to reinforce them. She seems to be composing as she goes—"as I have said above" is an acknowledgment she makes more than once—and as her list of instructions grows longer, her prose seems more hurried and less finished. And yet we can eventually discern the emerging pattern: as Anne compiles her list, she provides a series of lessons for each stage of Suzanne's life, examining, in turn, what is necessary for her as daughter, as wife, and as widow.[61]

To this end, she starts with the basics, just as her father had. He had begun his instructions with reflections on the transitory nature of this world, on the necessity of death, and on the eternal life of the soul. Anne's approach is similar. The "first and main point, more important than all others," is that Suzanne is careful "not to do, say, or think" anything that might anger God: "to live more chastely" and to protect herself from sin, she should always remember that not even one hour of life is sure. Contemplating the uncertainties of life,

---

[60]   By way of contrast, Louis IX compiled a list of only 21 precepts for his daughter, several of which are fewer than 25 words in length, the longest just over 100 words.

[61]   This conventional division reflects women's sexual status and their relationship to male authority. On the origin and development of this way of classifying women, see Carla Casagrande, "The Protected Woman," trans. Clarissa Botsford, in *Silences of the Middle Ages*, ed. Christiane Klapisch-Zuber, vol. 2 of *A History of Women* (Cambridge, MA: Harvard University Press, 1992), 70–104; see especially 73–84.

In constructing her City of Ladies, Christine de Pizan challenges such a division, proposing, instead, a three-part history of women illustrated with stories told by the allegorical figures of Reason, Rectitude, and Justice. Only as she draws her work to an end does she acknowledge the more conventional roles, addressing her final words to women who are married, to young women who are virgins, and to widows (see *The Book of the City of Ladies*, trans. Earl Jeffrey Richards [New York: Persea Books, 1982], III.19.2–III.19.5).

then, she should avoid those who waste their time in "vanity, delight, and foolish pleasure." To "better understand how to live and conduct [herself] with piety," Suzanne should occupy herself with a program of study, reading the books that her mother recommends. And because "idleness and daydreaming" are to be avoided, even while she is young, her mother advises Suzanne about other appropriate ways to keep busy; chess is fine, but playing games should never occupy too much time or become too important.

Anne is concerned with daughter's moral character. Suzanne must develop those virtues of particular importance for women, including chastity, humility, patience, courtesy, and modesty, and she must learn to practice them—her outward demeanor should always be carefully controlled, a reflection of these inner qualities.[62] She shouldn't make unseemly faces, shake her head, make eyes, smile too much. Because of her "weak female nature," she shouldn't even move "a single limb" of her body "without need." Anne also offers her daughter a great deal of advice about clothing. While she is young and able to wear them, she should dress "as custom dictates" wherever she is living. But, just as she is to be modest in her behavior, she should be modest in her dress. Anne warns her daughter against wearing anything that is too tight or too low-cut. And like any mother today, she warns Suzanne about dressing warmly rather than stylishly. "My daughter," she cautions, do not be like "those who, to seem more fashionable, dress themselves so scantily in winter that they are freezing with cold." Dressed so foolishly, they make themselves sick, and "many even die"; this is a terrible sin "because they have killed themselves."

---

[62] The seven fundamental virtues of Christianity include the "natural" (or "cardinal") moral virtues of prudence, temperance, courage, and justice (as defined by and inherited from the classical world), and the theological virtues of faith, hope, and charity (as defined by St. Paul). Each of the moral virtues has further virtues associated with it; temperance, for example, which includes abstinence, sobriety, and chastity, has "annexed" to it the virtues of continence, humility, meekness, and modesty. On this see *The Catholic Encyclopedia* [online], "virtue" and "cardinal virtues." On those virtues particularly important for women, see Casagrande, especially the section entitled "Women's Virtues and Vices," 84–104.

Despite Christian views about the equality of women's and men's souls, women's physical inferiority and her inherent weakness and instability were believed to require special vigilance and custody, and this control was the responsibility of men. On this, the first part of *Silences of the Middle Ages* is particularly helpful; see "Norms of Control," 11–158 (which includes three essays, Jacques Dalarun's "The Clerical Gaze," Claude Thomasset's "The Nature of Woman," and Casagrande's "The Protected Woman").

Much of her instruction thus constitutes a series of lessons for Suzanne to learn while she is young, although Anne is a firm believer in life-long learning, and later assures her daughter that "it is not a disgrace to be learning always." But she is also quite explicit about certain aspects of life for Suzanne while she is yet unmarried. She should be wary of men, who are always willing to promise anything in order to gain a young woman's confidence. She must never seek out private meetings, listen to the "blandishments" of love, or allow herself to be touched anywhere. The question of her marriage must rest with her parents alone. Suzanne should have no opinion on the matter, much less express one. If her parents both die before she is married, she should be very careful to place herself "in the service of a lady who is well regarded, who is constant, and who has good judgment."

As a wife and mother, Anne next advises her daughter how to conduct herself as a wife and mother. Marriage can be a "state of . . . beauty" that is "prized," but to achieve such a state, a wife can be neither too wise nor too patient. Once married, Suzanne should show her lord and husband "perfect humility" and "perfect love and obedience." She must not only please her husband but also his family and friends. She must ask for advice and then follow it. If God gives her children, she should pray that they are blessed with goodness and virtue—these are the first gifts a mother can give her children. She should teach them as well as she can, even while "realizing their limits as children." And Anne, the mother of a daughter, pays special attention to raising daughters since, as she tells Suzanne, they are "a heavy responsibility." Always self-aware, Anne insists that as a woman ages she should never compete with her daughter but, instead, "take up some gracious pastime." By the time a woman is forty, Anne observes tartly, no beautiful dress "can make the wrinkles on her face disappear."

Should she become a widow, Suzanne must neither give way to excessive grief nor move on without mourning. She must constantly remember that she has to set a good example for her children, and she must be aware of the particular dangers inherent in this stage of life—suspicions can arise because a widow must work closely with the men of her household. She should also be particularly wary of suitors and must take care to guard her reputation. She should maintain good relationships with family and friends, on whom she must rely. Suzanne must never be one of those "arrogant and foolish women" who think they are "wiser and more knowledgeable" than they really are; remember, Anne cautions, "you are not a fool unless you think you are wise."

Just as Anne seems prepared to draw her lessons to an end, she returns unexpectedly to where she began, addressing one further warning to Suzanne about preserving her virginity. Yet even after signaling that this "lesson" will be her last (Anne begins this section with a "finally"), she is unable to let go of the subject and adds still another "lesson" to her list, a reiteration of her discussion on the "virtue of chastity," this time accompanied by some practical suggestions on how to discourage would-be seducers. And then, suddenly, she has reached the end of her list and wraps up quickly: "And so," she writes, "to come to the conclusion of our discussion," when all is said and done, Suzanne must always remember that, in the end, she will die. In facing death without flinching, Anne both resembles her father and echoes him: "Those who live well," Louis wrote, "die a good death," and "whoever wishes to die a good death must also want to have a good life."[63] "Take great care to live well," is Anne's final advice to Suzanne, so that when death comes, she can face it without worry.

In focusing on the three stages of a woman's life and reinforcing social demands for women's chastity, silence, and obedience, Anne's lessons are entirely conventional. But in preparing these instructions for her daughter, in addressing them to Suzanne herself, and in assuming Suzanne's ability to embody and enact them, Anne of France also drew on her own unconventional life experience. Throughout her own life she exemplified the virtues and demeanor expected *of* women, even while transcending the limitations imposed *on* women. Her lessons reflect this doubled experience, and the result is a text as subtle and as shrewd as Anne herself. We will examine the way she negotiates these contradictions in the interpretive essay that follows our text.

Anne of France, *Madame la Vieille*

By the time she died at the age of sixty-one, on 14 November 1522, Anne of France had outlived all her contemporaries, and *Madame la Grande* had become *Madame la Vielle*, "the old Madam." Her brother had died in 1498, her sister in 1505. Isabella of Castile, with whom Anne had conducted business for eight years, died in 1504. Ludovico Sforza, who had lured her brother to Italy and who had tried to arrange for the marriage of one of his sons to Suzanne, died in 1508. Anne saw her one-time enemy Louis of Orléans succeed her brother as king of France; Louis died in 1515. Anne of Brittany, married first to Charles VIII and then to Louis XII, was also gone;

---

[63] *Rozier*, 9 and 10.

she died in 1514. And in what must have been a terrible series of blows, Anne's grandson François, born in July 1517 and named after his royal godfather, died within months of his elaborate baptism. Just a year later, Suzanne gave birth to stillborn twins.[64] Suzanne herself died in 1521, just thirty years old.

Her biographers have viewed the last months of Anne's life as a period of "darkness and despair": "She fell victim to the blows of a malady that remains mysterious to us," comments Pradel, a malady "doubtless fed by grief."[65] Matarasso concludes that "agony of mind and heart finished her off."[66] But another of Madam's formidable contemporaries faced her own losses and defeats with the unflinching gaze so characteristic of Anne herself. "I am habituated to grief," wrote Caterina Sforza, "I have no fear of it."[67] Surely Anne of France would have agreed.

---

[64] Pradel, 202–03.
[65] Pradel, 216.
[66] Matarasso, 288.
[67] Caterina Sforza (1462–1509) was regent of Imola and Forlì for her son; see Jansen, 38–53. She is quoted by René de Maulde la Clavière, *The Women of the Renaissance: A Study of Feminism*, trans. George Herbert Ely (London: Swan Sonnenschein & Co., 1905), 320.

In death as in life, Anne of France followed the model of her father. In his memoirs, Commynes notes that Louis XI "lived about sixty-one years, yet he always fancied he should never outlive sixty, giving this for a reason, that for a long time no king of France had lived beyond that age. Some say, since the time of Charlemagne; but the king our master was far advanced in his sixty-first year" (2:84). At the time of his death, Louis was actually aged sixty years, one month, and twenty-seven days (he was born 3 July 1423 and died 30 August 1483). His daughter was sixty-one years and some months old at the time of her death.

A Note on the Translation

In translating Anne of France's *Lessons*, I have relied primarily on the nineteenth-century edition prepared by A. M. Chazaud, who worked directly from the manuscript that belonged to Suzanne of Bourbon, but because the manuscript itself has now disappeared, I have also compared Chazaud's text to the first printed edition of the *enseignements*, published some time between 1517 and 1521. I have noted significant variations in the notes. My aim has been to produce a text that is readable, rather than strictly literal, while at the same time I have tried to preserve the distinctive voice of Anne herself.

Anne's prose presents a number of challenges for reader and translator alike. Beyond the erratic and idiosyncratic spelling, the "lessons" are filled with any number of grammatical problems—masculine and feminine nouns (and adjectives) are confused; pronouns, conjunctions, and prepositions are omitted; verb tenses change unexpectedly; and point-of-view shifts erratically. In his extended analysis of Anne's grammar, Chazaud lists many examples of *pléonasme*, or "redundancy," and *anacoluthes*, or abrupt changes in grammatical structures.[1] In other words, her prose is often filled with repetitions, and her "sentences" sometimes degenerate so completely that readers are apt to lose their way. I have silently omitted some of Anne's repetitions—she loves to pile point upon point with *et* or *car*, for example, joining phrases, clauses, and sentences with "and" and "because" at a dizzying rate—while still trying to maintain the hurried, almost unfinished feel of her prose. I have also struggled with some of the sentences, trying to untangle them without polishing her prose so smoothly that it does not resemble Anne's original at all—she is a well-educated woman, but not a professional writer, and her prose style reflects this. I must admit that in some places her syntax has defeated me; her meaning is clear enough,

---

[1] Chazaud's edition includes an extensive analysis of Anne's language, "Introduction Grammaticale," 261–300, as well as a glossary, 301–38, which is less useful, since Anne's vocabulary seems ultimately to have overwhelmed him (he spends more than two pages explaining the meaning of *accointance*, for example, but less than one page on all the words beginning with the letter *t*).

but the grammar of the sentence is not. I have indicated these spots in the notes so that Chazaud's original can be easily consulted.

Punctuation presents another set of problems. Chazaud's punctuation of Anne's text is confused and confusing, and it is unclear whether he is following the manuscript, supplying his own punctuation, or doing a little of both. The punctuation of the printed edition is not without its own problems, but it is generally much more systematic, and in many places it clarifies meaning that is confused in Chazaud's edition. Thus I have often followed the punctuation of the sixteenth-century edition, particularly where it indicates the end of one sentence and the beginning of the next and when its punctuation clarifies a confusion in the nineteenth-century edition. I have also modernized punctuation throughout.

Although Chazaud comments that Anne of France will never have "a place among the great French writers," I have found her to be sometimes witty, sometimes exasperating, but always engaging.[2]

---

[2]   Chazaud, 261.

Lessons for My Daughter

I

My daughter, the perfect natural love that I have for you—while bearing in mind our lamentable weakness and our present wretched life (innumerable and great dangers must be overcome in this transitory world), recognizing the imminent, sudden, and early death that I expect at any moment, and notwithstanding my poor, rude, and limited ability—gives me the desire and the determination to prepare a few little lessons for you while I am still with you, knowing well your inexperience and extreme youth and hoping that in time you will recall these lessons and that they will help you a little; therefore, without any long introduction and in few words:[1]

II

The first and main point, more important than all others, is that earnestly, and with all your faith and strength, you are careful not to do, say, or think anything that will make God angry at you.[2] So that no subtle temptations of the world, the flesh, or the Devil ever grab hold of you, then, and so that you live more chastely and protect yourself better from sin, always remember that, as Saint Augustine

---

[1] The formality and balance of Anne's opening section are notable, contrasting dramatically with the later sections of the work; on Anne's prose style, see "Introduction," 18 and 'Note on Translation,' 23–24. Anne uses the word *enseignements*, translated here as "lessons," to describe her instructions to Suzanne. According to Robert's *Dictionnaire alphabétique et analogique de la langue français*, the word *enseignements* means, in its first sense, a set of precepts that teach a way of living or a way of thinking; in its second sense, the word implies lessons drawn from experience. Certainly both meanings of the word apply to Anne's own "lessons" for her daughter. On precedents and models for Anne's *enseignements*, see "Introduction," 8–16.

[2] The most common verb Anne uses in her advice to Suzanne is *garder*, translated as "to guard (against)," "to take care," "to avoid," or, as here, "to be careful." Occasionally Anne uses the reflexive *se garder*, "to protect oneself," or *se garder de*, "to take care not to." Frequently (perhaps more often than not) Anne's advice is presented using the imperative form of the verb.

says, you cannot be certain of even a single hour; your wretched body must necessarily die, decay, and be eaten by worms, and your poor soul, left alone, will immediately receive her just reward for your life's efforts.[3] In the confines of your heart reflect constantly on the terrible, awful, and infinite pains of Hell, and on the great and inestimable glories and joys that are only in Paradise, fearing above all and in great sorrow of heart the dreaded day of universal judgment that very shortly awaits both the good and the bad. Remember Saint Bernard, who says that at every hour, wherever he is, he seems to hear the terrible sound [of Judgment Day] so marvelously strong he dreads it.[4] Alas! Now then, my daughter, consider those who are worldly and spend all their life in vanity, delight, and foolish pleasure—how can they ignore this sound when he, who was so perfect, feared it so greatly?

III

Next, my daughter, to continue our discussion, in great humility of heart consider and recognize who you are and what you come from: a pitiful and depraved creation when it comes to the body, excellent and noble when it comes to the soul which, as Saint Thomas says, is

---

[3]   In this sentence I have followed the punctuation of the sixteenth-century edition, which clarifies some confusion in Chazaud's edition.

    Saint Augustine Augustine of Hippo (354–430), one of the early Fathers of the Church and author of, most notably, *Confessions* and *The City of God*. According to an inventory completed in 1507, the Bourbon library at Aigueperse contained a copy of *The City of God* (in French); Anne's own library at Moulins, inventoried after her death, contained two copies of *The City of God* (one in French and another in Latin) as well as a Latin commentary on *The City of God* (on Anne's sources and the contents of the Bourbon and Moulins libraries, see "Introduction," 10–11).

    Anne refers here to "the soul" (*l'âme*, n.f.) with the feminine pronoun "she"; in translating from the French, I have preserved this usage.

[4]   *Saint Bernard* Bernard of Clairvaux (1090–1153), Cistercian monk and mystic. The library at Moulins contained a volume described as "*Le livre des lamentations sainct Bernard.*"

    the terrible sound [of Judgment Day] Anne's reference (*ce terrible son*) is to the sound of the trumpet that will herald Judgment Day: "And he will send out his angels with a loud trumpet call, and they will gather his elect from the four winds, from one end of heaven to the other" (Matthew 24:29–31; for similar references, see also Exodus 19:16, Leviticus 23:24, Psalms 89:15–17, Isaiah 27:12–13, 1 Corinthians 15:51–53, 1 Thessalonians 4:16, and Revelations 11:15).

created in the image and likeness of God.[5] Therefore, because of the soul's noble and unrivalled creation, and also because of the great reward we expect to have from her, we should rather die a thousand deaths if we must, as Saint Ambrose says, than abandon her even one time to sin as a result of our unchecked freedom.[6] Alas! Therefore, my daughter, we must consider well the many dangers, sorrows, and regrets that those poor and unfortunate obstinate ones must often have when they privately examine their evil and dissolute consciences. But, as Saint Bernard says, happy are those to whom God gives the grace, before their death, to have true and perfect knowledge. As the good philosopher Boethius says, this transitory life is very brief compared to that which will last forever.[7] And he also says that this world is nothing except deception, vanity, and temptation; very foolish are those who, no matter what, think to find perfect happiness here. Because, as he says, there is no one so powerful, so noble, or so free who is not weak, feeble, and subject. And he says that those who think they are wisest and know best are often the most foolish and the most abused and led astray. And he also says that a foolish hope of long life and too great a confidence in divine grace are both the work of the devil; because of them, we are blind in our hearts and deaf in our minds, deeds, and hearts. This is shown so clearly in so many places that it is obvious to all.

IV

And so, my daughter, take pride in nothing you think you have, not in your judgment, your strength, or your understanding, but always

---

[5]   *Saint Thomas* Presumably Anne's reference is to Thomas Aquinas (1224/25–1274), Dominican theologian and foremost Scholastic scholar, author of *Summa theologica* and *Summa contra gentiles*, canonized in 1323. The Bourbon library contained a volume described as "*Le livre De tribus virtutibus theologicis sanctis Thome . . . de Acquino*" (which seems to be an extract from the second part of *Summa theologica*, a discussion of the three theological virtues, faith, hope, and charity) while the Moulins library contained *Cathena aurea sancti Thome* (*The Golden Chains of Saint Thomas Aquinas*, his commentary on the Gospels).

[6]   *Saint Ambrose* Ambrose (c. 339–397), bishop of Milan. The library of Moulins contained a copy of Ambrose's *De officiis ministrorum*, on the moral obligations of the clergy.

[7]   *Boethius* Anicius Manlius Severinus Boethius (c. 470–524), the Roman author of *De consolatione philosophiae* (*The Consolation of Philosophy*), one of the most influential books of the Christian Middle Ages. The Bourbon library

live in great fear and on your guard so that you are not deceived, and
avoid idleness, especially in your mind. Occupy yourself always with
good works, for example reflecting with great devotion on the holy
and dignified Passion of our sweet savior Jesus, rendering Him
thanks and praising Him kindly.[8] And to better understand how to live
and conduct yourself with piety, I counsel you to read the small book
of the noble Saint Louis and that of Saint Peter of Luxembourg; read
The Book of Vices and Virtues, Wisdom's Watch upon the Hours, or
other books of the lives of the saints; and read also the sayings of the
philosophers and ancient sages, whose teachings should be a true rule
and example for you.[9] Such reading is an honest occupation and a

      contained two copies of the *Consolation* (one of which seems to contain only the
      prologue); the Moulins inventory also notes a copy of the work.

[8] *Occupy yourself always with good works, for example, reflecting with great
      devotion on.* . . . The sixteenth-century edition here reads, ". . . reflecting with
      great devotion on the commandments of God and on the articles of the faith, and
      on the holy and dignified Passion . . ." (sig. A5v).

      Passion Anne refers here to the suffering, death, and resurrection of Jesus
      Christ; in addition to the importance of Jesus' Passion as part of the Church year,
      it was an important topic for devotional works. Both the Bourbon and Moulins
      libraries contained several volumes on the Passion story, in both prose and verse.

[9] Not all of Anne's specific references here are clear. In beginning her reading list
      for Suzanne, Anne recommends *le livret* (small book or notebook) of Saint
      Louis, presumably Louis IX (1214–1270), king of France from 1226–1270,
      leader of the Seventh Crusade to the Holy Land, canonized in 1297. The king's
      instructions to his son, *Les Enseignements de saint Louis à son fils,* may be the
      book to which Anne refers (see "Introduction," 14); Louis also addressed some
      enseignements to his daughter Isabel, queen of Navarre (printed by Chazaud,
      xx–xxvii). Neither the Bourbon library nor the Moulins library inventories list
      such a "small book," but the instructions to his son are interpolated into some
      versions of *The Chronicles of France* and *The Chronicles of Saint Louis,* copies
      of both of which are inventoried.

      The second *livret* Anne recommends to Suzanne (*celui de sainct Pierre de
      Luxembourg*) may refer to the Moulins volume inventoried as "*Examen de
      conscience de sainct Pierre de Luxembourg.*"

      The next volume on Anne's reading list, *The Book of Vices and Virtues,* is a
      manual of moral and religious instruction written by the Dominican friar Brother
      Laurent in 1279 for Philip III of France, the son for whom Louis IX wrote his
      enseignements; Anne refers to this book by its French title *La Somme le roi*
      (literally, "the sum the king"—Anne writes *les sommes le roi*). Among the
      work's contents are explanations of the Ten Commandments, the Lord's Prayer,
      the Seven Deadly Sins, and the articles of faith. There is no volume on either the
      Bourbon or Moulins inventories with this specific title, but the Bourbon library
      volume inventoried as *Les Sommes* must surely be this work.

      Anne also recommends *Wisdom's Watch upon the Hours* (*Horologium
      sapientiae*), a dialogue between the author, the Dominican Henry Suso

pleasing pastime. Furthermore, concerning your youth: you must not waste it in idleness or daydreaming, but keep busy and occupy yourself honorably but not too eagerly in pleasant games like chess, tables, merels, or other such minor amusements, nothing too novel or that requires too much attention.[10] The minds of some women are

(c. 1300–1366), and Divine Wisdom. Inventoried in Moulins library is *L'Orologue de Sapience*, a French translation of Suso's work.

In recommending Suzanne devote her attention to "other books of the lives of the saints" (*aultres livres de vie des Saincts*), Anne directs her daughter to a genre well represented in the Bourbon and Moulins libraries; over twenty separate books contain either collections of saints' lives (such as the Bourbon *La Vie des Sainctz*, for example) or volumes dedicated to individual saints (Catherine of Siena seems to have been a particular favorite, with several different versions of her life in the two libraries).

When she advises Suzanne to find a model in "the sayings of the philosophers and ancient sages" (*les dictz des philosophes et anciens saiges*), Anne might be referring to individual philosophers and their works (volumes of Aristotle, Augustine, Thomas Aquinas, and Albertus Magnus, for example, were in the Bourbon and Moulins libraries), but more likely she is referring to a composite work like the four-volume collection of *sentences* ("sentences," sayings or maxims) found in the Bourbon library (which may be a copy of the fifteenth-century collection compiled by Guillaume de Tignonville).

[10] Chess seems to have been a favorite occupation of Anne's family (her grandfather Charles VII was said to have been addicted to chess, which may in part account for Anne's caution about devoting too much attention to games). Among the books in the libraries of Bourbon and Moulins were three separate volumes on chess. One is simply described as "the book of chess" (the Bourbon library's *le livre des eschesz*, bound in leather), but two others focus on allegorical uses of the game; one may be a French version of Pope Innocent III's "morality of chess" (the Moulins copy of *Le livre des moralitez du jeu des eschetz* had originally belonged to Charlotte of Savoy) and the other may be a version of the Dominican Jacobus de Cessolis' fourteenth-century *Liber de moribus hominum et officiis nobilium* (the Moulins volume is entitled *La moralité des nobles hommes et saiges, selon le jeu des eschetz*). For a brief but easily accessible account of these medieval allegories using the game of chess, see Johanna le Mercer [Jo Anne Fatherly], "The *Innocent Morality*: Chess from Sermon to Romance"; http://www.geocities.com/Athens/Pantheon/7756/murray.html; Internet; accessed 12 June 2003.

The second of the "pleasant" games Anne recommends is "tables," or backgammon. The word "tables" referred to the board (table) on which the game was played and, by extension, to the game itself. The Moulins inventory notes that a "beautiful square marquetry table" made in Germany, perfect for games like backgammon, was in the library at the time of Anne's death. As an interesting note, a 1457 inventory made of the Bourbon *hôtel* in Paris includes two game tables, a walnut marquetry table *à jeu de tables*, and a second marquetry table *à jeu d'eschez* (Jean-Marie de la Mure, *Histoire des Ducs de Bourbon et des comtes de Forez en forme d'annales sur preuves authentiques . . .* , ed. R. Chantelauze [Paris: A. Montbrison, 1868], 2:247–48 nn).

occupied so completely by such things that they have neither the strength nor the understanding to think about anything else, which is not a sign of good judgment or of good manners in a woman of rank.[11] Such things should be employed in moderation; they are an appropriate way of passing the time instead of doing nothing. As Doctor Lienard says, all women who wish to have a good reputation and be recognized as worthy should have their hearts, their wills, and their minds so wholly raised on high that their principal aim is always focused on the acquisition of virtue.[12] As a certain philosopher says, our most profitable endeavor, the greatest and most noble treasure

Finally Anne recommends the game of *marelles* to Suzanne; today this French word refers to the game of hopscotch, but Anne is referring to "merels," another board game. For an introduction to this very popular medieval board game, see Ron Knight, "Merels"; http://www2.kumc.edu/itc/staff/rknight/Games.htm; Internet; accessed 15 April 2003.

Excellent information on all three games, complete with illustrations from medieval and Renaissance manuscripts and books, is Karen Larsdatter, "Medieval and Renaissance Games and Gaming Equipment"; http://www.geocities.com/karen_ larsdatter/games.htm; Internet; accessed 15 April 2003.

[11]   *woman of rank* Throughout her *enseignements*, Anne refers to *femmes de façon*, literally "women of fashion." Since "fashion" has a very different connotation in modern English, I have translated the phrase here as "women of rank."

[12]   *Doctor Lienard* The identity of Doctor Lienard has eluded readers of Anne's lessons including, most recently, Pauline Matarasso, who refers to him as "Madame's favourite authority, a certain doctor Lienart" (*Queen's Mate: Three Women of Power in France on the Eve of the Renaissance* [Burlington, VT: Ashgate Publishing, 2001], 192). This intriguing figure is certainly the authority Anne refers to most frequently; the key to his identity is provided by Alice Hentsch, *De la Littérature didactique du moyen âge s'adressant spécialement aux femmes* (Cahors, France: A. Coueslant, 1903), who notes that Anne is referring to Leonardo of Udine, an Italian preacher and Dominican prior in Bologna (199). The always amazing *Enciclopedia Universal Illustrada Europeo-Americana* (s.v. "Leonardo d'Udine") adds a few further details: that he was a popular preacher and that his *Sermones aurei de sanctis* was published in Venice in 1473, several years after his death (c. 1469). Further research has added a few more details—he is Leonardo di Matteo of Udine, born about 1400, a doctor of theology (which accounts for Anne's reference to him as *Doctor* Lienard); his *Sermones aurei de sanctis* ("golden sermons on the saints"), a series of sermons on individual saints and on the life of Christ, the Virgin, the Holy Spirit, and the Holy Trinity, were composed and preached in 1446; his 1434 Lenten sermons, preached in Florence, were printed as *Quadragesimales sermones de legibus* (Ulm, 1478); a third book, *Prediche*, was published in Venice in 1492. What is very interesting, however, is that despite Anne's many references to him, no book attributed to him is listed in the Bourbon and Moulins inventories. (Could a Moulins volume entitled *Sermones dominice orationis* refer to a collection of his sermons?)

that we can ever seek to acquire, is the salvation of the soul, the ultimate glory of the body.[13]

V

And so, my daughter, devote yourself completely to acquiring virtue.[14] Behave so that your reputation may be worthy of perpetual memory: whatever you do, above all, be truly honest, humble, courteous, and loyal. Believe firmly that if even a small fault or lie were to be found in you, it would be a great reproach. As Doctor Lienard writes in his argument about lying, it is the worst of all the vices, foul and dishonest to God and the world.[15] Now then, my daughter, if you would like to be numbered among worthy women and to have a good and honest reputation, be very careful to avoid it. And as Socrates says, do not be like those foolish idlers who, in their idiocy, think themselves wise and worthy when they deceive and abuse many people with their evil and venomous cunning, which is detestable to God and abominable to the world.[16] And as the aforementioned Doctor Lienard says, no man or woman of great rank who has good judgment wants to have such a reputation. And he also says there are many dishonest and evil nobles in the world today who come from good families and have a large following, but, to speak frankly and truthfully, those who follow them are either fools or have business with them. Be assured, as the aforesaid doctor says, that if their followers flatter them to their faces, they damn them behind their backs. Finally, as Saint Ambrose says, whatever pretences they make and however long it takes, in the end such people are neither

---

[13] Throughout her *enseignements*, Anne cites "a philosopher" or "one philosopher," perhaps drawing from a volume like the one she recommends to Suzanne as *les dictz des philosophes et anciens saiges*, n. 9.

[14] *devote yourself completely to acquiring virtue* Here, as throughout her lessons, Anne stresses the importance of Suzanne's moral character, her development of virtue; see "Introduction," 19.

[15] Although library inventories do not include a book attributed to Doctor Lienard (see n. 12), here Anne clearly refers to a written source. A literal translation of her original reads: "Because, as Doctor Lienard says in an argument that he makes where he is speaking about lying . . ." (*Car, comme dit le docteur Liénard, en ung argument qu'il fait ou il parle de mensonge . . .*). This brief reference indicates something about Anne's process of composition—she has read and studied the works she cites.

[16] *Socrates* The Greek philosopher Socrates (b. c. 470–399 BCE), whose life and works are preserved in the dialogues of Plato.

loved by God nor the world. Wise men say you should fly from them as if they were poison no matter how pleasing their greetings and no matter how charming their pastimes—in the end, associating with them is too perilous. And so, my daughter, protect yourself from them and their deceptive company.

VI

In addition, my daughter, if it so happens that death takes me before you have been provided for and it turns out that, with the counsel and advice of our lords and friends, you are taken to court or to some other great house, whatever you do, at least if it is possible, place yourself in the service of a lady who is well regarded, who is constant, and who has good judgment.[17] As Doctor Lienard says, there is no terrible vice in anyone that cannot be corrected, tempered, or eliminated by this noble virtue. A certain philosopher says no man or woman with good judgment, either in history or in literature, was not, in the end, honest and good and worthy of memory—whatever their other faults and despite the faults of those whom they saw or spoke to or with whom they were involved.[18] Another philosopher says that it is unfortunate for any land where the lord is an infant, a judgment that can also be made about fools. On this same subject, another philosopher says that it is the greatest misfortune in the world when a wise man is subjected to the government of a fool. And so, my daughter, protect yourself, as you can, from being so subjected, because, as Doctor Lienard says, it often happens that even the best followers and attendants are blamed and then punished for the great mockeries, unexpected mistakes, and crazy enterprises their foolish masters and mistresses undertake out of their own unreasonable desires and without any

[17]   *lady* In her recommendation to Suzanne that she place herself "in the service of a lady," Anne writes, *mectez-vous en service de dame ou demoiselle*; these two words, *dame* and *demoiselle*, indicate a distinction in the rank or age of the "lady" whom Suzanne might serve. According to Robert's *Dictionnaire*, the word *dame* refers to a hereditary title with a right of sovereignty or suzerainty, while the title of *demoiselle* is used either for a young noblewoman or for the wife of a lesser nobleman.

   great house Anne uses the word *hôtel* here; as defined by Robert, the *hôtel* was the town house or mansion of a great lord. I have generally translated the word as "great house"; on occasion I have used "castle" or "household."

[18]   Anne's syntax here is very confused, but her point is clear.

good or appropriate counsel.[19] For this reason, then, you should avoid serving such people because no good can come of it. But if it happens that you find yourself in such a situation, you must exert all your efforts to helping them see their faults and to admonishing them, not by confronting them, reprimanding them, or correcting them, but subtly, sweetly, and lovingly, by proposing something new, for example, or by making a pleasant suggestion or by praising the suggestions of others or by showing your approval of some other action or deed, always returning to the just and moral truth by reminding them very gently that when all is said and done, death is inevitable, and, therefore, it is good to learn how to live well so that, when the time comes, they will know how to die well—but avoid lengthy explanations because it is not the custom of such people to willingly hear about or to speak of death.

VII

And although this subject may be necessary and appropriate, and something about which you should speak frequently and readily, especially to your friends, nevertheless it is not good to speak about it too often for fear of boring them, which you do not want to do. Whoever they are, you must please them while you are in their service—that is, serve them in what is reasonable and in nothing else. As Doctor Lienard says, you should not be like those many foolish flatterers who, to gain a little credit, a little influence, or a small reward, praise and approve every notion of those whom they serve, lauding them, sympathizing with them, lying to them, or agreeing with them, whether what they propose is wrong or right, and never urging their support for anything reasonable, honorable, or right, or against anything, even when it is brutish or damned. Saint Paul says that such foolish people deny the faith and are much worse than infidels and,

---

[19] *followers and attendants* Throughout her instructions, Anne uses the words *serviteurs* (n.m.) and *servantes* (n.f.) to refer to members, male and female, of an aristocratic household. In both Alain Rey's *Dictionnaire historique de la langue française* and Robert's *Dictionnaire*, these words are interchangeable, meaning "one who serves," but since the English word "servant" implies someone who is a domestic worker, I have used "attendant" when Anne refers to a *servante* (female) and either "follower" or "member of the household" when she specifies a *serviteur* (male).

    masters and mistresses The words here (*maistres ou maistresses*, as Anne writes) refer to the lord or lady of the great house.

accordingly, they can neither suffer nor bear too great a trial or punishment.[20]

VIII

For this reason, my daughter, whatever mistress you serve, be careful not to become like those foolish attendants, no matter what; rest assured that, however long it takes, in the end they are sure to repent, either in this world or the next. As Boethius says, God is perfectly just and, however long it takes, He leaves nothing unpunished. Also, my daughter, with regard to the court, it is not right for a young woman to meddle in or busy herself with too many things. Wise men say that you should have eyes to notice everything yet to see nothing, ears to hear everything yet to know nothing, and a tongue to answer everyone yet to say nothing prejudicial to anyone. And they also say that it makes no sense to inquire after every bit of gossip and that strong desires are always suspect. According to one philosopher, those who have good judgment know how to protect themselves from such desires. Nevertheless, those who have little sense try hard to fulfill them, and for this reason, after you have given every possible service to your mistress, I advise you take care to please all others according to their rank; honor them appropriately, especially those who have great influence and who are said to be wise, while at the same time preserving your conscience, honor, sincerity, and loyalty.

IX

In addition, be humble to all, to the lowly as well as the great, be kind, courteous and amiable, and be truthful and temperate in all things. And if it happens that, out of envy or hatred, someone speaks out against you or speaks falsely about you or your honor or something else, suffer it patiently, seeming to think nothing of it and

---

[20] *Saint Paul* There are several saints named Paul, but the most likely reference here is to the apostle Paul (d. 68/67). The inventories of the libraries at Bourbon and Moulins note several copies of various parts of the Bible, some of which must have contained Paul's epistles; in addition, the Moulins inventory notes that Anne had two copies of the New Testament and at least two copies of the epistles, one of which was in Greek and Latin. The Bourbon library also contained a life of Saint Paul.

always remaining pleasant. As Doctor Lienard says, anger and envy
are never so great that they cannot be softened by the virtues of
kindness and humility. Further, take care to tell no tales to anyone at
all, because sometimes even those who do so justly, with reason and
good intentions, are later hated for it and suffer a great deal.[21] And
so that all goes smoothly, I counsel you to mind your own business,
without asking about anything or wanting to know anything about
the affairs or conduct of others. And if by chance it happens that you
know something, take care that you do not reveal it; although someone may ask you about it, do not admit to knowing anything. As
Socrates says, a man or woman of great rank should never reveal the
secret of another as long as there is no harm in concealing it and
especially as long as it does no harm to your master or mistress. If
there were anything dishonorable, such a thing should not, of course,
be concealed, but privately, as if you were making a confession and
not some other way, you should inform your master or your mistress's confessor.[22] As I told you above, even what is said or done
with the best of intentions is not always appreciated.

X

Also, my daughter, concerning your clothing and headdress, I am
satisfied that, while you are young and can do so, you dress yourself
as custom dictates in the place where you are living and at the pleasure of your mistress.[23] Always make sure that you dress as well and

---

[21] Chazaud begins a new paragraph with this sentence, but the sixteenth-century
edition makes no break at this point. I have followed the printed edition here.

[22] *confession* "Confession" is part of the sacrament of penance (see *The Catholic
Encyclopedia* [online], "the sacrament of penance"), the entire ceremony often
called simply "confession"; aristocratic women like Anne and Suzanne would
have their own private spiritual counselors who would function as their "confes-
sors." Anne is advising her daughter to reveal only what might be to the disad-
vantage of her "master" or "mistress," and to reveal this only to someone whom
she can trust to act discreetly.

[23] Fashions were very extravagant in the late fifteenth century, and Anne's concern
for her daughter's attire seems to reflect more than her desire for moderation in
all things. Here she begins her recommendations about Suzanne's *habitz et
atours*, a topic which she will return to several times later in her work. The word
habits is familiar from the English "habit," and is translated here as "clothing,"
but the word *atours* is less familiar. The word can refer generally to "attire" or
"array," but Anne's reference here is to a woman's headdress. Like other items
of women's attire, headdresses could be very extravagant; Christine de Pizan

as neatly as you can because, in the eyes of the world, you must understand that it is unseemly and distasteful to see a young girl or a woman who is nicely dressed but untidy.[24] No man or woman of rank can be too carefully dressed or too neat in my opinion, provided that their clothing is not too outlandish or so important to them that they forget to serve God. And Doctor Lienard says that it is good to pray often to God in order to avoid any temptations that might arise from this cause. He strongly recommends that, in addition to your other prayers, you say three Our Fathers in the morning, on rising, and as many Hail Marys, the first time thinking of the grievous Passion of our redeemer Jesus, the second thinking of His great humility in deigning to descend to the depths of Hell for no other reason than to comfort His friends, the third thinking of the inestimable joy of His glorious mother on seeing Him resurrected.[25] These three Our Fathers, said morning and evening, will help protect

cautions women to avoid extreme fashions in their headgear as well as in their clothing (see, for example, *Treasure of the City of Ladies*, II.11). Information on medieval apparel is readily found on the Internet; a well-researched, well-documented, and fully illustrated site is Alianora Munro, "The Wardrobe"; http://members.aol.com/_ht_a/noramunro/Wardrobe; Internet; accessed 8 April 2003 (the site illustrates the *atours* with an image of a miniature from the Hours of Mary of Burgundy).

    in the place where you are living Here Anne uses the word *pays*, understood today as meaning "country," but which can also be used to indicate "region" or "area." Given the fifteenth-century setting for Anne's text, I have avoided the twenty-first century connotations associated with word "country."

[24] It is difficult to determine exactly what Anne is objecting to here. She writes: *Car au regard du monde, croiez pour vray qu'il est mal séant et fort deshonneste de voir une fille ou femme noble nicement habillée et mal en point.* In particular, the phrase *mal en point* (*mal empoint*, in the sixteenth-century edition) presents the difficulty. In his version of Anne's text (see "Introduction," n. 43), Joseph Viple seems to understand the phrase as *en pointe*, that is, a caution for Suzanne to avoid a "plunging" neckline (a bit of advice Anne is more explicit about in Section XI), but given the context here, where she is concerned with neatness and tidiness, I think the phrase should be understood as a caution against being "untidy" (see Robert's *Dictionnaire*, where *point* can refer to a "spot" and which translates *mal en point* as "in a bad state"). I should note, however, that much about fifteenth-century fashion was "pointed"—the atours (which could be very tall), deep v-necklines, long and fluttering sleeves, and long, pointed shoes, for example—so Anne might be talking about any number of extravagant fashions.

[25] *three Our Fathers* Following Doctor Lienard's advice, Anne recommends that Suzanne repeat the *Paternoster* ("Our Father") *trois fois* ("three times"). The Lord's Prayer appears in two forms in the New Testament, Luke 11:2–4 and Matthew 6:9–13.

    as many Hail Marys Anne also recommends the *Ave Maria*, composed of the three "salutations" addressed to the Virgin Mary: "Hail, Mary, full of grace, the

you from all temptations.[26] For this reason, my daughter, it is good to get used to saying them often.

XI

But to be brief and to return to our topic, clothing, I counsel you not to wear anything outrageous, either too tight or too trailing, nor should you resemble those women who think they are very fashionable when their clothing is low-cut and very tight and they attract attention; they think their dress is admired, for which they are mocked and rightly reproved by those who hear the talk.[27] Nor, my daughter, should you be like those who, to seem more fashionable, dress themselves so scantily in winter that they are freezing with cold, their complexions often sallow and without color, until, either because of the cold they suffer in private or from being too tightly laced, they endure many grievous illnesses, and many even die—never doubt that this is a great sin because they have killed themselves.[28] And ignorance is not an

---

Lord is with Thee, blessed art thou amongst women" (the greeting of the archangel Gabriel, Luke 1:28), "Blessed is the fruit of thy womb, Jesus" (the words of Elizabeth to her daughter, Luke 1:42), and "Holy Mary, Mother of God, pray for us sinners now and at the hour of our death" (added during the fourteenth or fifteenth century).

   the inestimable joy of His glorious mother on seeing Him resurrected One of the "Seven Joys of Mary" (which include the Annunciation [Luke 1:26–38], the Visitation [Luke 1:39–45, 56], the Nativity [Luke 2:1–7], the Adoration [Matthew 2:1–2, 9b–11], the Finding of the Lord in the Temple [Luke 2:41–51], the Resurrection [Luke 24:1–8], and the Assumption [widely accepted as doctrine by the end of the Middle Ages, but not declared official dogma of the Church until Pope Pius XII's *Munificentissimus Deus*, 1 November 1951]). The libraries at Bourbon and Moulins contained many volumes devoted to the Virgin, including several on her life and several on the miracles associated with her.

[26] Anne refers here specifically to the repetitions of *Ces trois paternostres*, not to both sets of prayers.

[27] Again, some of Anne's admonitions about clothing are not clear. For example, she cautions Suzanne not to wear any *habillements* that are *fort chéans* (which Viple translates as *fort tombants*); I have translated the phrase as "too trailing." In telling Suzanne not to be like "those women" whose clothing she dislikes, Anne describes them as *font ouvertes*, which Viple translates as *elles sont très décolletées*; following his suggestion here, I have translated the phrase as "low-cut," referring to the clothing itself, not the women.

[28] Anne's distaste for tight clothing (which she returns to in Section XIV, below) reflects a fashion concern of the fifteenth century, when lacing became very popular. This is not a reference to a nineteenth-century style corset, but to various efforts to "mold the torso into a cylindrical shape, and to flatten and raise the

excuse in such situations because, as the Philosopher says, if you are not wise, you should seek counsel from or follow the example of those who are.[29] And Doctor Lienard says that those who would be wise exercise moderation in such things and are orderly and measured without being obliged to be so and without making fun. You must always suit your manner to your person and your rank. It is fitting for everyone—and especially so for noblemen and noblewomen—to bear themselves well and honorably and to have a kind manner, well-regulated and assured in all things. And because of their weak female nature, it is especially important for all women of rank who want to have a good reputation to be so shamefast and fearful of bad judgment that they move not a single limb of their body without need and that they be rightly ordered with a kindness always compassed by reason.[30] On this subject, one philosopher says that the most displeasing thing in the world, especially for men of rank, is to see a young woman from a good background who is unpredictable and unrestrained. And on the other hand, as another philosopher says, the most noble and pleasing treasure in this world is a woman of noble rank who is beautiful, young, chaste, and well-mannered.

bustline." Again, the Internet offers immediately accessible, well-documented, and well-illustrated resources; see, for example, Drea Leed, "History of the Elizabethan Corset" (quoted here); http://costume.dm.net/corsets/history.html#; Internet; accessed 8 April 2003.

[29] *the Philosopher* The Greek philosopher Aristotle (384–322 BCE) became "the Philosopher," the "Master of Those Who Know," in the Middle Ages. Anne had access to several works by the Philosopher, including a Bourbon volume described as *ung livre d'Aristote*, as well as several volumes in the Moulins library, including an Aristotelian text entitled *De animalibus*, which may be one of Aristotle's works on animals (*The History of Animals*, *On the Parts of Animals*, *On the Progression of Animals*, or *On the Generation of Animals*); two copies of his work described as *"le livre de l'espèce,"* but not further identified; and two three-volume copies of his *On the Heavens*. A book described as *"quatre volumes d'ethiques et politiques et yconomiques"* might represent Aristotle's work on ethics and politics.

[30] *because of their weak female nature* Both classical and Christian views of women stressed their inherent weakness and men's consequent responsibility for guarding and controlling them; on this see Carla Casagrande, "The Protected Woman," trans. Clarissa Botsford, in *Silences of the Middle Ages*, ed. Christiane Klapisch-Zuber, vol. 2 of *A History of Women* (Cambridge, MA: Harvard University Press, 1992), 70–104, in particular her discussion of "submissive custody" (89–91). Here Anne acknowledges this view of women as naturally weak even while asserting that women whose actions are determined by reason are capable of controlling themselves. She makes a similar point earlier, in Section VI, when she assumes that "women with good judgment" may, like their male counterparts, control and eliminate vice.

XII

And so, my daughter, because virtues and good works are as well praised, loved, and valued in this world as they are in the next, you should take great pains to be virtuous; to this end, make sure that your conversation is always honest and good, that you are courteous and amiable in all things, and that you are pleasant to all and loved by all. And, truly, when it comes to love, the Philosopher says honesty must be its foundation because any other "love" is only false treachery and hypocrisy—with all the authority and power that a mother can and should have over a daughter, I command you to flee from such love. It is important to control your bearing, your expressions, your words, your sentiments, your thoughts, your desires, your wishes, and your passions. As Saint Paul says, of all the temptations and subtle deceptions in the world, this is one of the worst, and from "love" comes great evil, so dishonestly is it practiced today. As many doctors agree, there is no man of worth, however noble he may be, who does not use treachery, nor to whom it does not seem good sport to deceive or trick women of rank from one good family or another, it doesn't matter which. And Doctor Lienard says there is no man so perfect who, in matters of love, is truthful or keeps his word, however firm or fervent—which I certainly believe. One time I heard a noble woman of great rank tell about a knight she knew who, in such a situation, took a solemn oath of his own free will, on his honor as a gentleman, on the altar and on a missal where Mass is said everyday—and this knight did not keep his oath for more than four hours![31] And, as she told me, the oath was very reasonable and, with all respect to his honor and conscience, he had no excuse whatsoever for breaking it except his own lust, weak will, and sudden change of heart.[32] Therefore, my daughter, whatever

---

[31] *knight* Anne describes this faithless man using the phrase *gentilhomme* [gentleman] *et chevalier.* According to Robert's dictionary, the word *chevalier* is a feudal title designating a fief sufficient to support a mounted soldier, and thus the English word "knight" is used here.

   Mass The celebration of the Eucharist; the term "Mass" comes from the priest's dismissal at the end of the ceremony, *Ite, missa est* ("Go, it is ended"). The service includes the liturgy of the Word, including readings from Scripture and a sermon, and the liturgy of the Eucharist, which includes the offertory, a Eucharistic prayer, and the Communion.

[32] Although there is no paragraph break at this point in the sixteenth-century edition, Chazaud begins a new paragraph after this sentence.

flattering speeches or great signs of love that someone may make you, trust none of them. As Doctor Lienard says, those who are wisest and think they are following the right path are often the first to be misled. And he also says that because of their own sense of loyalty and morality, they think to find the same in the deeds and words of others, and for this reason they are often deceived. And the said doctor also reminds us that God has no reason to ensure that your steadfastness, honesty, and loyalty will find their like; you must question whether such love, which should be principally for Him, is right and proper.[33] Although, certainly, it must be said that when those of virtuous character come together, by one means or another, love can be marvelously great and, in the end, good and honest. But when this does happen, as Doctor Lienard says at the end of his argument about true love, the enemy, who is full of venomous subtlety, uses his power to break and distance such love because of the great goods and honors that result from it.[34] As I have told you above, my daughter, do not trust in the chastity, strength, or perfection you think you perceive in yourself or in someone else; on the contrary, know that not one in a thousand escapes without her honor being attacked or deceived, in one way or another, however "good" or "true" her love. Therefore, for the greatest certainty in such situations, I advise you to avoid all private meetings, no matter how pleasant they are, because, as you have seen, many an honest beginning comes to dishonest and harmful end. And even when it seems all is for the best, you must also fear the foolish and the irresponsible opinions others often express, to the prejudice of women and at their expense. As Doctor Lienard says, in this situation and in others, the world is so vile and so corrupt that true love is hardly understood or recognized. As another philosopher says, a praiseworthy thing is never recognized by those who are neither experienced nor virtuous; for this reason they often judge that which never was. Consider, then, that many women have suffered a great deal and some have lost their honor and advantages, even in marriage. But that is another subject, and I will not lengthen this lesson by discussing it with you here.

---

[33] Anne's syntax in this sentence is very confused; in his version of the *enseignements*, Viple avoids this passage altogether, neither quoting it nor translating it into modern French. While the grammar of the sentence is unclear (and the translation offered here may thus be incorrect in some details), Anne's point is, nevertheless, quite clear—while love for any man is uncertain (God has no reason to ensure the beloved will be worthy of a woman's love or that the beloved will return her love), love for God is always certain and certain to be returned.

[34] *the enemy* Anne here refers to Satan, the "enemy" of both God and humanity.

XIII

Therefore, my daughter, if you would be wise, fly from and eschew all such dangers, fearing the evils that can result from them. And to speak to you of marriage: it is a state of such beauty and so prized, provided it is honestly regulated, that it seems as if it cannot be honored enough or praised too much. And to achieve this state, you cannot devote yourself to it too much or conduct yourself too wisely or with too much gentleness, deference, and chastity, in manner as well as in deed, and you should not have any preferences, desires, or wishes of your own, nor do anything on your own or according to your own desires, but depend on the prudence, good grace, and judgment of your friends. A certain philosopher says that she who does otherwise is a complete fool. For this reason, my daughter, put these things in your memory and conduct yourself so wisely that you never miss any happiness that it pleases God, of His goodness, to send to you.

XIV

Do not be like the three young ladies of long ago, daughters of the very noble and very powerful lord of Poitiers. These young women were so exceptionally beautiful that they were renowned throughout the world, and they were, therefore, sought by many in marriage, in particular by three noble and powerful princes from the region of Germany who, because of the reputation and fame of the three young ladies, were very much in love with them.[35] And secretly, with little fanfare and without one knowing about the intentions of the other,

---

[35] This delightful story is one of the most appealing parts of Anne's lessons to her daughter. Anne identifies the beautiful young women as *trois demoiselles* (see n. 17), and their father as *seigneur* [lord] *de Poitiers*. The city of Poitiers is now the capital of Vienne, in west central France; the province was part of the dowry Eleanor of Aquitaine and passed to England on her marriage to Henry Plantagenet (1156); it returned to the French later in the century, was then won back by the English at the battle of Poitiers (1356), then reconquered by the French in 1374.

The young nobles who come to see women they have heard so much about are described as coming from the *païs d'Alemaigne et marches d'environ*, that is, they come from "the country of Germany and its surrounding marches" (border or frontier).

they all three arrived in Poitiers on the same day at the same hour, and so it was that they encountered one another and told one another why they had come there—that is, to see the aforesaid young ladies for themselves. So powerful were their desires they could not rest without seeing these girls. The lord of Poitiers was informed of this news, at which he was very happy, and he quickly went to them and brought them to his castle, where they were honorably feasted by the lady of Poitiers and her three daughters. It so happened that the oldest was very tightly laced and so constrained by her clothing that her heart had been weakened, as she revealed to the first prince when he questioned her.[36] He was very unhappy at the sight of her in such danger and wanted to know the reason; after he was told why, he knew that this had happened because of her arrogance and foolishness. It seemed that, because of this weakness, she would never be able to bear a child, and he concluded in his heart that he would never be able to marry her. The second prince intently regarded the bearing and manner of the second daughter; he found her to be so unpredictable and unthinking that he took her for a fool, so he also concluded that he could never marry her. The third prince was drawn to converse with the youngest daughter, whom he found completely astonishing, speaking to him so boldly, especially about love, that he judged her both foolish and unchaste, and he would rather have died that very hour than ever marry her.[37]

Thus were the three young girls exposed, my daughter, in the way that you have heard, and so they lost their happiness through their follies. The princes immediately took their leave and hastily departed with few words, except that the youngest could not go without saying something to the lady, the mother of these girls, about his "nice" introduction to her daughters and the "gracious" conduct he had seen in them—the meeting had been an honor, worthy of remembering always. The lady understood his words as well as their meaning; she was so embarrassed and so unhappy that she no longer had any joy in life and died not long afterwards. For this reason, my daughter, heed this example and, wherever you are, avoid making any unpleasant faces and shaking or turning your head this way and that, and do not stare, peer around you, or let your eyes wander. Also, make sure you do not laugh too much for any reason because it is

---

[36] In her story about the three daughters of the lord of Poitiers, Anne returns to the issue of tight lacing, which she discussed explicitly in Section XI, above.

[37] Although there is no paragraph break at this point in the sixteenth-century edition, Chazaud begins a new paragraph after this sentence.

very unbecoming, especially for young noblewomen, whose manners should be more solemn, gentler, and more controlled than the manners of others.[38] Nor should you talk too much or too sharply, like many foolish and conceited women who want to attract attention and, to be more admired, speak boldly and in a flighty way, responding to everyone and on all topics, which is very unbecoming in all women, whatever their state, but especially so for young virgins, rich and poor alike, who must protect their reputations.[39] Because of their careless talk, many young women are judged to be foolish and unchaste; as one philosopher says, the way a woman minds her eyes and her tongue is an indication of her chastity.[40] For this reason, my daughter, always use your eyes and tongue cautiously and carefully; that is, know when to speak and where your eyes belong, never be the first or the last to talk, and do not be a tale-teller, especially of something unpleasant or prejudicial. Also, be slow and cool in all your responses because, as wise men say, on some subjects a reply cannot be avoided. Also, take care not to run or jump, and do not pinch or hit anyone. Likewise suffer no man to touch your body, no matter who he is, no holding of hands or pressing of feet. In conclusion, my daughter, remember those three aforementioned daughters who were the cause of their mother's death, and do not behave so that your bad conduct is the cause of mine.

XV

I could address many other lessons, explanations, and comments to you on this topic, but to be brief and to further our discussion: if it turns out, my daughter, that by the grace of God you marry into some great and high estate or are married to a lord of great power, guard yourself well from becoming too proud or arrogant because you should always maintain your humility. As Doctor Lienard says, in this miserable world no great lord or powerful prince has any

---

[38] On the noblewoman's role as a model for other women, see Casagrande, 78–79.

[39] Anne's recommendation is for all *jeunes pucelles*, "young virgins," whatever their social class.

[40] From the Middle Ages through at least the late seventeenth century, women were enjoined to be chaste, silent, and obedient. Of particular interest is the connection between silence and sexuality—that is, a woman who guards her tongue is also judged to guard her sexuality, while a woman who is free with her tongue is judged to be sexually free as well. (This association is seen in Christine de Pizan's *Treasure of the City of Ladies*.)

reason to be proud if he understands clearly the terrible danger and utter subjugation he will shortly face; if great lords and powerful princes wish to acquit themselves loyally for the many benefits and blessings that they owe to God, they should regard their great seignories and benefices as heavy burdens, terrible restraints, and dangerous worries that must, at all hours, be present before their eyes.[41]

XVI

Now then, my daughter, since it is true that you are a feminine and weak creature, you should take good care that, whatever good fortune you have, you conduct yourself graciously, in perfect humility, especially to your lord and husband, to whom, after God, you owe perfect love and complete obedience; you cannot be too humble or bear him too much honor, and you should serve him in all of his needs and should always be sweet, obedient, and amiable to him as well as to all his relatives and friends, each according to his or her degree, because there should be order in all things. That is to say, you owe more honor to the father and mother of your husband, if they are still living, than to any of his other relatives, and more to a brother than to a cousin, and so on, honoring each according to his or her place in his family; serve each member of your husband's family properly, just as you serve each member of your own. Remember that whatever great alliance you achieve, you must never out of some foolish pride fail to value highly your own ancestors, those from whom *you* are descended—to fail in that would be against right and reason.[42] According to Doctor Lienard, those who fail to do so are like Lucifer who, through his pride, wished to elevate himself above God his creator and compared himself to Him. Through his own arrogance, he fell from the highest, most excellent, and noblest place in Paradise to the stinking and abominable pit of Hell, taking many of his band with him.[43] Know then, my daughter, how greatly we must fear incurring the anger of God

---

[41] *seignories and benefices* A "seignory" is the domain or estate of a lord; a "benefice" is a feudal grant, a fief.

[42] *against right and reason* (*contre droict et raison*) The sixteenth-century edition reads "against God [*Dieu*], right, and reason."

[43] *Lucifer* Lucifer (from the Latin "light-bearer") was the name of Satan before his fall; he was cast out of Heaven for his pride in thinking himself to be God's equal (see Isaiah 14:12–20).

for this accursed sin of pride, for which the most beautiful and the noblest angel in Paradise suffered eternal punishment.

XVII

Many foolish women have so little understanding that being seated above their own mothers or grandmothers seems to be a glory and honor, and they think nothing of their great-aunts or their older sisters, much less of their position or their honor, nor do they consider their connections or lineage, nor the rank and family of their husbands.[44] I have seen more than one such "noble" woman acting arrogantly in front of her mother and grandmother, not showing them any honor or even speaking to them; do not offend anyone, or those who witness your behavior will deride you for it. This happened once when a niece, a simple lady of little moment who was married to a mere knight, advanced herself to take precedence over her aunt, who was noble and respected. The young woman was then disparaged, and many took her for a fool.[45] As Doctor Lienard says, there is no better way for women to demonstrate their folly than, through their own pride, to debase those from whom they are descended, those whom, by reason, they should honor and love. Although their alliances are scarcely so grand that they have even the slightest reason to advance themselves, if by chance such women find themselves in the unusual situation where, because of the honor or nobility of their alliance, there is no one in a position of greater rank than themselves, they should rather take a place behind other women than to offend them and their families. But when the place of honor comes to them, they should accept it with great humility so that everyone knows that they have not taken it presumptuously or thoughtlessly. You can be certain that those who so conduct themselves earn great glory and renown and, as a result, will have even greater honor. And also God said in the Gospels that those who humble themselves will be raised and exalted, and so, my daughter, whatever advancement you might have in this world, if you wish to acquire an honorable reputation, guard yourself always from the presumptuous vice of pride, and

[44] Anne's point is clear, although her syntax is not.
[45] A person's rank is illustrated by precedence—that is, a person's status is indicated by where she sits at the table, for example, or who enters a room first. Here Anne calls "foolish" a young woman who presumes to take precedence over other women in her family, thus failing to show them any respect or honor.

know that it is not a desirable thing—nor is there a better way to earn people's love than to be humble, kind, and courteous.[46] Saint John "the Golden Mouth" says that these are the principal virtues worthy women ought to have; he also says, by contrast, that the evil and damnable vice of pride is, of all the vices, the most displeasing to God and the world, and that now great envies and evils come from it.[47] Another philosopher says that there is no woman so wise who will not fall into the sin of pride, lose her reputation, and, in the end, be taken for a fool if she fails to apply herself and act other than according to right and reason. But in this situation as in others, I believe you must act with measure and reason; nobility should never be degraded or weakened.[48] In this and similar situations, the greatest should always try to advance others, without displaying the favoritism or pretense that so many do now. Because of their insatiable greed, they often favor others rather than their own close relatives; in their

---

[46] *God said in the Gospels that those who humble themselves will be raised and exalted* Anne's reference here is to the so-called Beatitudes (see Matthew 5:3–12), part of Jesus' Sermon on the Mount (Matthew 5:1–7:27; see also Luke 6:17–49). The sixteenth-century edition differs from Chazaud's edition here: "And also Our Lord Jesus Christ said in his Holy Gospels that those who humble themselves will be raised and exalted, and those who exalt themselves will be humiliated" (sig. B9r).

[47] *Saint John "the Golden Mouth"* Anne's reference is to John Chrysostom (b. c. 347–407), archbishop of Constantinople, one of the early Fathers of the Church whose preaching earned him the surname "Chrysostom," or "Golden Mouth." His homilies, particularly on the Gospels of Matthew and John and on St. Paul's letters, established his reputation; these seem to be represented in Anne's library at Moulins, which contained two volumes described as *Omelie Johannis Crisostomi* and *Traductio librorum Johannis Crisostomi, super Matheum, e greco in latinum.*

   these are the principal virtues worthy women ought to have On the virtues associated particularly with women, see "Introduction," 19. In contrasting these virtues to vices, and in particular to pride, Anne alludes to the Seven Deadly Sins, and to the "contrary virtues" that are their opposites: humility opposes pride, for example, as generosity opposes covetousness (or greed), chastity opposes lust, kindness opposes envy, abstinence opposes gluttony, chastity opposes lust, patience opposes wrath (or anger), and diligence opposes sloth. See also n. 73, below.

[48] *I believe you must act with measure and reason* Here, as elsewhere, Anne's advice reflects Aristotle's notion that virtue represents the mean between extremes (Anne may have had a copy of Aristotle's *Nichomacean Ethics*; see n. 29, above). While always acknowledging women's "weakness," Anne nevertheless assumes that they have the good judgment, the "measure and reason" to find the way between extremes and, therefore, the ability to act "according to right and reason."

arrogance, they advance others over noble and gentle women, even when these worthy women are members of their own families.[49] If you are acting with reason, you must never do this because no worthy woman should be rebuffed or degraded, especially not on the authority of those who, in this situation as in others, should be honoring them. And so, my daughter, notwithstanding the gossip, hatred, and envy that are often the result of preserving or protecting your own rights, I counsel you to show the greatest courtesy and humility you can to others, even those of humble origins, giving them every honor, without reproving them or displeasing them in any way, but if it happens that you must constrain them to preserve your own position, do it so graciously and in such a kind manner that no one in this regard will have cause to judge you badly. As one philosopher says, nobility cannot be denied by the arrogance of a mere woman. And another philosopher says that high birth, without nobility of heart, is like a dry tree without foliage or fruit, or like wood that burns without giving off any heat.[50]

XVIII

For this you should know: nobility, however great, is worth nothing if it is not adorned with virtue. Therefore, my daughter, you must always have the heart of a noble woman, and if you wish to have a good and honorable reputation, always exhibit virtue and prudence in all things. Take care not to be caught off guard, whatever rudeness you encounter. Know that those who seek to advance themselves this way actually fall further behind; they publicly recite their honors, status, or lineage, which might otherwise go unrecognized, but this is the very reason why they were not sufficiently honored in the first place. Noble and good women, on the other hand, are glorified, valued, and honored by everyone—and by the wise in particular—for

---

[49] Anne's syntax is very confused here.

[50] *high birth, without nobility of heart* Here and in the section that follows, Anne distinguishes between nobility of birth, an accident, and "nobility of heart," a characteristic of moral character. The topic was very popular in the fifteenth century, the distinction between nobility of birth and "true nobility" explored in many texts, among them *The Instruction of a Young Prince* (*Instruction d'un jeune prince*), two copies of which were in the library at Moulins. For a discussion on late fifteenth-century texts in particular, especially those in French, see Charity Cannon Willard, "The Concept of True Nobility at the Burgundian Court," *Studies in the Renaissance* 14 (1967), 33–48.

their virtuous patience, their humility, and their great constancy. Many lords and ladies wish to advance and support those who are not noble rather than those who are, but true nobility, wherever it is found, can never be defaced or erased.[51] As Doctor Lienard says, no one of worthy and upright heart, against all reason, wants to befoul nobility and pull it down. And if it happens, my daughter, that you have a great castle or a large household, take care that you do not show favoritism or dissimulation, but show loyalty, constancy, and truthfulness to all, preserving everyone's right and giving everyone good council, as you are able, when it is required of you. And if you see any lady or any other honest woman of your own household who is unhappy or melancholy, take care to offer her sweet words that will recall to her the tribulations and sufferings of those who love God. Remind her as well of the great good that we will acquire if we have patience in our adversities—patience is a work of great merit, very pleasing to God, and through it we earn great renown. And Doctor Lienard says that it is one of the best ways a woman can demonstrate her great virtue. For this reason do not just pretend to have it.

XIX

Furthermore, my daughter, you must attend to other women in times of childbirth, misfortune, and illness and, if you have it, send them something you think they might need or that might please them; you should do this at the very least for the women you know, especially for your own relatives and those of your husband, because whether they are poor or rich, you owe them more than anyone else, as long as they conduct themselves honestly.[52] Today many lords and ladies fail to take care of members of their own families, even though they are wise and well-regarded and have done them no dishonor, just because they are not influential people. And some are so arrogant and presumptuous that they willingly deny members of their own family, who are hurt when they hear about it, but these proud lords and ladies act as if they know nothing about it, for example changing the subject when

---

[51] *lords and ladies* Anne writes *seigneurs, dames ou demoiselles*, again indicating a distinction in age or rank in the women about whom she writes.

[52] *in times of childbirth* Anne refers to *gésines*, that is, the preparations that precede, and the rituals associated with, childbirth; her library at Moulins contained a volume entitled *La gésine nostre Dame*.

they are asked about their prejudice, which is against reason and shows their evil and damnable nature. Never doubt that those who behave in such a way will be punished, in this world or the next, for their terrible sin. Such people are like the infidels who deny our faith—they deny their own blood and lineage, which they should love, advance, and honor above all and to the last drop. On this very topic a certain philosopher says that no men or women of good judgment will let their head be swelled with the folly of pride. For this reason, my daughter, flee from it above all else, thinking always about the ultimate truth, which will give you true knowledge of this deceitful world—which is, to speak truthfully, a thing of no importance. Saint John Chrysostom says those to whom God has given the grace to put into effect this true knowledge are happy; for this reason, my daughter, employ your understanding and act so that you will be loved by God and the world. Acquire that sovereign grace which will enable you to follow the right path. After that, my daughter, to gain earthly grace and to have a good reputation, always be truthful, be humble, firm, and gracious in all your actions, and be gentle when you are in the presence of others, especially at Mass, which you should hear with great devotion and always on your knees, if it is possible, having your eyes always intent on the priest, on the altar, or on your book, without looking around you during the service. In the same way, do not fiddle with your hands like other young girls, who, out of a foolish habit, always have their hands at their nose or at their mouth, at their eyes or at their ears, which is very unbecoming, especially for noblewomen who, surely, are more watched than other women—and for this reason they need to be more careful. Noblewomen are, and should be, a mirror, a pattern, and an example for others in all things. On this topic, a certain philosopher says that there is no fault in any noblewoman so small that it is not very displeasing to all worthy people who see it. For this reason, my daughter, as well as for many other more obvious reasons that it would take too long to list, never set a bad example for anyone or behave in a way that can result in slander instead of good, and take care to please everyone; thus no one will have reason to hate you. In addition, speak humbly to the small as well as to the great, and treasure their small offerings and presents when they give them, considering them more costly and worthy than even the greatest of gifts. You should never fail to reward them and thank them humbly, kindly, and clearly, without any affectation or falsity, because if you fail to do so, you will be mocked, and it will be said to be a sign of arrogance, not wisdom, and that will be all the reward you will have. Affectation is never becoming in any woman, but it is especially unbecoming in married women; they rightly have more influence than others in all things and thus should be more honest, whether in speaking or anything else. Many women, by speaking too much, make a spectacle of themselves because their speech is frenzied, dishonest, prejudicial, or out of season.[53] Such women should not be numbered among noblewomen of worth—you should flee from their company as from poison because, as Cato says, a woman's greatest virtue is her restraint of her tongue.[54] But neither is it good for a woman of rank to be dull or too silent because, as Ovid says, such a woman, whatever other perfection she has, is like an idol or a painted image, and in this world she is only a mere shadow, a faceless number, an incumbrance.[55] For this reason, my daughter, take care to speak kindly, to respond graciously, to converse about honest and pleasant subjects, and to be agreeable to all, according to their rank. To the devout, speak about morals and about those things that are profitable to the soul; to the wise, speak moderately about honorable subjects. To help the young and joyous avoid melancholy and pass the time, you should sometimes arrange for new and charming stories to be told or for pleasing words that will make them smile and enjoy themselves. To the householder, talk about household management.[56] You should also honor those from foreign lands whether they come to see you in your establishment or whether you encounter them elsewhere. You should attend to them first, before anyone else, and converse with them, asking them about the customs, laws, and habits of their land, for example talking with them about the lords and ladies of their land and praising them, and during your

---

[53] Anne's syntax here is very confused; this translation depends on the emendation made by Chazaud, 67.

[54] *Cato* Anne's reference is to Publius Valerius Cato (fl. 1st c. BCE), Roman poet and grammarian. None of the books in the Bourbon and Moulins libraries seems to be a volume of Cato.

[55] *Ovid* Anne's reference is to Publius Ovidius Naso (43 BCE–17 CE), Roman poet. Ovid's work is well-represented in the Bourbons and Moulins libraries, whose inventories note a copy of the *Metamorphoses*, a book entitled *Les fables d'Ovide*, and two additional volumes, one simply described as *Ung Ovide*, the other as *Le livre d'Ovide, du duc de Berry.*

[56] *To the householder* One of the conduct books suggested as a model for Anne's *enseignements* is the fourteenth-century *The Householder of Paris* (*Le Ménagier de Paris*), written by a citizen of Paris for his fifteen-year-old bride (see "Introduction," 12–14). The book entitled *De gouvernement de manger*, one of the volumes in the Bourbon library, may be a copy of the Householder's conduct book; in any case, Anne's familiarity with Christine de Pizan's advice on running a household (in *The Treasure of the City of Ladies*) would provide her with plenty to talk about on the subject of "household management."

conversation, make sure you are as pleasant to them in your questions as in your responses. Also, my daughter, in traveling from one place to another, wherever it may be, acknowledge the people of the towns and the lesser folk graciously, inclining your head toward them so that they have no reason to think badly of you, because if you wish to have a good reputation everywhere, you must please the small as well as the great, because from such people come both renown and slander.[57] For this reason it is good to have their love—and there is no better way to gain their love than through humility. Speak to them graciously about their husbands, wives, children, and households, comfort them in their poverty, and admonish them to have patience because to those who are patient come gifts of charity, and from patience comes both the grace of God and the world; for this reason, spare neither your efforts nor your words, which in this situation are appropriate and beneficial. And, my daughter, because good words are loved and valued by everyone, take care that you are not gloomy, sad, or pensive, and do not be one of those who, through pride or disdain, does not deign to speak to anyone or speaks so low that you can scarcely hear them—it seems that every word they speak either costs them dearly or causes them great pain, and this is a very foolish affectation. The greatest gift that God has given to us is the gift of speech, and He is most aggrieved when we use this gift badly, speaking too much or too little; either one is unbecoming, especially to those whom you should fear, love, and obey, like your father, mother, older family members, or other great lords and ladies. Therefore, my very dear daughter, although your natural condition is to speak little, you should always make an effort to speak with and respond courteously to those with whom you will conduct business.[58] And wherever you are allied by marriage, good or bad, high or low, act always so that you will earn God's love and the goodwill of others. Nor should you be melancholy or discomfited if you find yourself in some foreign or unpleasant alliance, but praise God and believe that He is always just and never does anything but what is reasonable. Therefore, my daughter, if it is so ordained and it

---

[57] *the people of the town and the lesser folk* Anne refers to *les simples gens et menu peuple.*

[58] *my very dear daughter* Here the sixteenth-century edition adds the "very dear" (*très chiere,* sig. C4r) to Anne's usual "my daughter."

although your natural condition is to speak little Anne's comment here may well mean that, as a woman, Suzanne should "speak little," but this sentence seems almost to suggest that Suzanne's nature is to be relatively quiet—and thus her mother advises her to overcome her natural diffidence and "make an effort" to speak to others when speech is appropriate.

happens that you have much to suffer, have complete patience, finding in whatever awaits you the will and pleasure of the Creator. Also, never openly reveal yourself by any outward sign, semblance, or circumstance, or by your relationships, or by any other means; if you want to live with peace of mind, protect yourself from stumbling into the snares of jealousy. Even if there is just cause, known to everyone, you must always bear it patiently, seeming to know nothing, as much for the love of God as for the honor of your husband; do not be melancholy but give thanks to God and praise Him for it while praying with all your heart that it will please Him to remove this folly and to have pity on your husband's soul. And with great ardor, my daughter, so that you have the greatest reason to thank Him in your adversities, reflect carefully on your birth, on the certainties of life, and on the end of all pleasures and joys.[59] Whoever considers these three subjects will have more reason to wish for hardship than ease: as bitter and difficult as life may be in the beginning, so in the end it will be sweet. The contrary is also true, but, either way, it is necessary to have patience. Boethius addresses this when he says that nothing in this world is so bad but that some good will come from it and that worldly pleasure is, in the end, damnable. He also says that God, who is the ultimate good, allows those who love Him to suffer for several reasons: first, the better to test their patience, so that they will achieve greater glory; second, to purify them, so they will be like martyrs; and third, to eliminate their evil desires and joy in worldly pleasures, so they may have knowledge of His great majesty and His own suffering.[60] For this reason, if we have perfect good sense, we would rather have tribulations in this world than anything else, because such trials and adversities are the means to Paradise—but only if we have patience.

XX

Therefore, my daughter, to gain the great joy and glory of Paradise, give thanks and praise to God with a full heart in all your adversities,

---

[59]   *on your birth* Anne's advice to Suzanne is, literally, to think "on the origin of your birth" (*la cause de vostre naissance*). It may be that Anne wants Suzanne to reflect on her own lineage, or it may be that she wants her daughter to think on her "origins" as a human being, one of God's creatures. Given the following sentence, I prefer the latter meaning (see also the similar injunction in Section III).

[60]   *martyrs* The libraries of Bourbon and Moulins contained several volumes on the lives of Christian martyrs, those who suffered and died for their faith.

believing that, like many others better and more perfect than you, you will have many more if it pleases Him. This is why you have no reason to defy anyone, especially your husband. You owe him nothing less than compliance and obedience so that you do not provoke his folly; God and the world expect nothing less of you. Likewise you should have no greater care than to earn the love of his lords and friends as much to avoid the blame wives often, but unjustly, suffer for the bad government of their foolish husbands as the better to please your husband; to earn and deserve his love and that of his friends, conduct yourself wisely and chastely not only in your actions but your words, because a woman who is not chaste is careful about what she does and nothing else. Also, when you are in the company of others, act demurely, in harmony with their desires, doing what you think will be agreeable to them and taking their advice in your affairs without doing anything on your own. To arrogant women it seems a shame and dishonor to ask for and follow advice—do not be one of these fools. When those who should give them advice and counsel say something to them or remonstrate with them about what relates to their benefit or honor, they take it very badly and do not consider this advice, sometimes doing the opposite or even worse! And there are some so wicked that they would rather follow the advice of their followers or some renegade neighbor than more honorable counsel. As one philosopher says, those who ignore the counsel of their friends believe more readily that of their enemies, which often harms them—afterwards they repent, but it is too late. The same philosopher also says that those who abandon their friends lose and exile their own good and honor. For this reason, my daughter, stay close to your friends, taking their advice and, as you can, helping them with their interests and necessities. When these friends are foreign or of great rank, you must always do your duty and graciously help them conceal their faults; you cannot blame them even a little without it becoming a grievous burden on the soul and a great dishonor because, according to a certain philosopher, whoever reveals what should be concealed commits a mortal sin. Thus you must take care because no good can come from such behavior.

XXI

Moreover, my daughter, guard against idleness in yourself and in your women because idleness is the devil's daughter and leads women to perdition.[61] She engenders not only the sins of the flesh but all other vices as well.[62] For this reason you must avoid her with all your might, and you must protect your attendants from her as well, especially your women, who must always be maintained in diffidence and obedience or they will do only what pleases them, without any consideration for their mistress, who will be blamed. To suffer such blame is a great dishonor for any woman of rank, because under the shadow of such sufferance, many will come to false conclusions about the whole situation, usually about the mistress herself. It might be thought, for example, that she is hiding some secret or her women would never dare to behave as they do. For this reason you must never suffer idleness in your women. You should not allow them to be rude or willful either, nor should you reprimand them too little because that is what foolish women do.

XXII

And so, my daughter, if your women do not behave as they ought to, show them their faults sweetly, using few words.[63] As the proverb says, great substance often resides in a few words—or, a few short words to the wise and even fewer to those who stubbornly persist in their perverse and accursed views and are thus incorrigible.[64] For this reason you waste your time thinking to chastise them; there is no remedy unless you give them leave and dispatch them immediately. It is folly to retain such people, as it is to hold onto the sharp-tongued, the tale-teller, the quarrelsome, and the liar, because there is a danger that someone may listen to them, often to the detriment of their master or mistress. Never trust such people, and if you find them around you, send them away graciously. In addition, you must always maintain a blameless and honorable household; do not suffer blameworthy followers or bad conduct or anyone whose honor has

---

[61] *leads women to perdition* (*meine dames à perdicion*) The sixteenth-century edition reads "leads the soul (*l'ame*) to perdition." Idleness is a particular danger for women, given their weak and imperfect natures, because it endangers their chastity; see especially Casagrande, 96–98.

[62] Anne refers to "idleness" (*l'oysiveté*, n.f.) with the feminine pronoun "she" (*elle*); I have preserved her usage.

[63] *their faults* The sixteenth-century edition reads "their follies (*leurs folles*) and faults."

[64] *As the proverb says* The inventory of the library at Moulins lists a composite volume containing *Les Proverbes moraulx*.

been tarnished, especially women; always keep a close watch over them, and never allow them to make fun of or speak falsely about others, but make certain they are obedient, diffident, well-ordered and well-ruled, each appropriate to her rank as is fitting in a well-run household, and always set them a good example, both for your honor and their profit.

XXIII

Next, my daughter, in order to attain the lofty and honorable reputation that gentlewomen must have—and so that no one ever has any reason to hate you—guard yourself above all against the deadly sin of envy. Many weak-willed fools are envious of everyone, but especially of women who are accomplished and of great rank; so great is their arrogance that envious women cannot listen to, praise, or value women who are good and without flaws. The more beautiful a woman is, or the more she knows, the greater is the evil in their minds and the more their hearts are inflamed. When someone honors and praises virtuous women, the envious, out of spite, speak ill of them. Some women are so poisoned by envy that when they see good in other women, even one of their own relatives, they hate them so much that they revile them everywhere they go, which greatly displeases God. And as Saint John "the Golden Mouth" says, envious women must be considered like those who, out of envy, betrayed and crucified Jesus. Because of their damned envy, these women with treacherous hearts betray and murder those whom, in God's eyes, they should love, and they destroy the honor and profit of the virtuous as well. There is no greater treason in this world than to defame and dishonor someone secretly, out of envy. It is the condition and nature of the envious that, if they cannot satisfactorily revenge themselves on those they envy, then they want them dead or have them killed—and thus they are revenged. But they arrange this so no one is aware of it, because such people only act covertly and foully, and in their malice use subtle means so that they do not discover themselves to honest people and so that the honest do not see their machinations.[65] The envious contrive great falsehoods about the

---

[65] *such people only act covertly and foully* I have preferred the reading of the sixteenth-century edition here, which describes the actions of the envious as *couvers et infectez*; Chazaud's edition here reads *couvers, et en faincte*, perhaps meaning that the envious "act covertly, using dissimulation."

goodness and honor of those whom they envy, and simple people believe their lies and spread them, certifying them to be true; thus it comes to pass that the honor of many is damaged for no reason, all because of envy. Therefore, my daughter, make sure you are not thus surprised and, likewise, do not suffer envy in any of your women because it is the sin that is most often the reason for speaking ill of others, a fault that has no equal. No family of any prince or any lord can be said to be good or honorable if it is touched, even once, by envy. For this reason, above all, avoid the company of the envious—if their company is pleasant at the beginning, in the end it will be evil and dishonest.

XXIV

Moreover, my daughter, make sure you do not mock anyone, and do not suffer mockery among your women because it is dishonest and a sign of poor understanding. Now it often happens that those who are mocked are better and more virtuous than those who mock them. A noble heart must not taint itself with such an evil stain; rather, you must look at and examine the state of your own life before amusing yourself by making fun of others. You must also consider whether your mockery can be turned against your own family because you will, in turn, be criticized by others. Nor will anyone have any reason to make fun of others once they have carefully considered themselves and their own situation. Know then, my daughter, that those who are the best and most virtuous are those who most often have to guard themselves against failing and who must excuse the simplicity of the ignorant: not all are equal in knowledge, either because of a fault in their understanding or in their experience. So, my daughter, if you have knowledge, praise God and correct the faults of your subjects kindly, without mockery, because in the end mockers are mocked.

[25][66]

And if someone tells you it is just natural to mock others, it shows that person is a natural fool, and if this mockery is habitual, that

[66] In the sixteenth-century printed edition, a new section begins at this point; on the structure and numbering of Anne's *enseignements*, see "Introduction," n. 58.

shows the mocker associates only with malicious people. Or it might be the result of youth, with no evil intended, but it should still be considered folly when it harms others. For this reason, my daughter, guard yourself and those of your household from mockery, because it is the work of malicious people. And if you have some followers who do not wish to obey you in this, dismiss them immediately because it only takes one with this fault to spoil all the others. Therefore do not suffer them but govern them sagely and discreetly so that they have no cause for disobedience and no reason to lessen their obedience to you. Also, show them that you are their mistress not only in your bearing, manner, and demeanor, but also in your headdress, robes, and other clothing. You must always have the best when it comes to your attire; it should be richer than that of any of your women. Their clothing should never resemble yours; it is badly done if you allow this, because such extravagant habits are not to be praised. In all things the mean is virtuous, and for this reason I counsel you to hold to it, whatever abundance of goods and honors you have, so that you will not anger God with your pride. Dress in the fashion of your husband's land and at his pleasure, without any affectation or undue care, always conducting yourself honestly and maintaining in your women, according to their rank, obedience, diffidence, humility, and kindness, without suffering them to do anything that is not honest.[67] You must also ensure their devotion and, whatever happens, make sure they serve God, hear the Mass every day, observe the Hours and other devotions, pray for their sins, go to confession, and frequently give alms.[68] And to console them and enliven their youth, and the better to maintain their love for you, you must sometimes let them frolic, sing, dance, and amuse themselves happily but honestly, without groping, hitting, or quarreling. And, to avoid melancholy, you must take pleasure in their company and

[67] Although there is no paragraph break at this point in the sixteenth-century edition, Chazaud begins a new paragraph after this sentence.

[68] *Mass* On the Mass, see n. 31. Noblewomen like Anne and Suzanne (and the members of their households) would be expected to attend Mass daily.

    Hours "Hours" refers to the canonical hours, the tradition of prayers at Matins (daybreak), Prime (early morning), Lauds (morning), Terce (mid-morning), Sext (noon), None (mid-afternoon), Vespers (evening), and Compline (night). While the Hours and the office of their celebration were the responsibility of priests and monks, Books of Hours were personal prayer books of the laity. The inventory of Anne's library at Moulins notes a Book of Hours that belonged to "Madam," with which she said her Hours (*pour dire ses heures*).

    alms The offerings of charity to the poor and needy are "alms."

converse with them graciously, but not with too much familiarity or intimacy because it is very dangerous to do so—sometimes you speak against yourself and, later, you regret it. As the Philosopher says, those who have their secrets hidden have them imprisoned, but if they tell their secrets then they themselves are in prison. And rest assured that if you tell your secret to anyone else, even your best friend, she will think afterwards that you should be more obliging to her than you were before; some people think that when you trust them you will never dare correct them or do anything without consulting them.[69] If it comes to pass that at some point you break off your acquaintance with them, they grow to hate you—you, who trusted them—and they will tell everyone the secret you shared with them, and out of spite they will say the worst things they can, and it will not trouble them at all to talk about what they know. The world today is corrupt in this regard, so you do not know whom to trust. Although those who are noble should never be so vile, it nevertheless seems today that the power to betray or reveal someone's secret is considered to be a fine thing by many nobles (noble, that is, by birth, but not by nature).[70] We can see for ourselves that they take pleasure in doing this and think to acquire renown, even when the secret belongs to someone worthy; they think they will be considered wise if they know the counsel of those who are important. Therefore, my daughter, be very cautious about those in whom you confide, and do not reveal to anyone what you should conceal because rarely is love perfect and completely untainted and disinterested, and, among a thousand, rarely is there even one who will serve another solely out of love and without some more practical consideration, whatever it may be. And so, my daughter, conceal that which can affect your honor, and if it is something that it strains your heart to conceal, and if it seems to you that it would be better to talk to someone and seek counsel, consider well to whom, and how, you reveal yourself; it should be someone in your husband's family, or your own, who are all worthy people, because they will have more reason to conceal what you have confided in them than other people. But, my daughter, whatever their relationship to you, and although it seems as if they will conceal your confidence, you must always cherish them dearly and please them, and you must not be rude to them

---

[69]   *some people think* The sixteenth-century edition reads "you ought to know that some think" (*devuez sçavoir que alcuns cuydent*).

[70]   *noble, that is, by birth, but not by nature* On this distinction, which Anne has addressed before, see Sections XVIII and XIX and n. 50.

or show them any sign of mistrust, because this is the main reason why many reveal the secrets of others.[71] If by chance there is a reason to distance yourself from them or mistrust them, you must always behave graciously so that no one, least of all they themselves, perceives it, for fear it will make more trouble. You must clearly see that you cannot govern too wisely with kindness and diffidence. Also, you must do the same when others do you the honor of entrusting you with something important because their confidence is a sign of their love for you, and there is no better way for them to show it. For this reason you must use all your power to comfort them and counsel them loyally, concealing what they have confided and excusing them for it to everyone, because you must never allow another person to be blamed in your presence, whether you are the most important person in the company, or the least; you must excuse yourself and speak of some other, happier, matter.[72] For, my daughter, you are more strongly obliged to excuse those who confide in you than others, although their love and confidences are very dangerous and fearful and you have no certainty in this changeable world. This is why those who are wise do not want to know the secrets of others, but fear to know them. Nevertheless, when you know something, you must acquit yourself loyally and believe that your care in safeguarding the mistakes of those who are bad will serve as an example of your caution to those who are good.

XXV [26]

Moreover, my daughter, so that you are always loved more and better by everyone, always be humble and gracious, especially to those people who come to visit you. Converse with them kindly, without assuming the haughty or distant manner of some women who behave like proud princesses to those who come to see them, never condescending to take even one step when their visitors arrive or when they depart, though their visitors are often more noble and virtuous than the women who receive them; such haughty women are often mocked for their behavior, and worthy people distance themselves from them. For this reason, my daughter, always be ready to honor everyone in

---

[71] *sign of mistrust* (*signe de defiance*) The sixteenth-century edition reads "sign of childishness" (*signe d'enfance*).

[72] *some other, happier, matter* The sixteenth-century edition adds "some other *more pleasant*, happier matter."

your household, especially women who are noble and worthy; take great pains not to belittle nobility because those who denigrate it reveal their negligence. Know also that great knowledge is never without virtue, from which nobility derives: nobility is found there, in virtue, first. Because of their virtue, you thus cannot honor the knowledgeable too much. If you do them a favor, they will double it in return, honoring you and spreading your renown wherever they go; it is good to be on pleasant terms with such people and not to be like those foolish women who annoy them and make them angry for nothing. Also, my daughter, do not be so inconstant or fickle that you become bored with worthy people and, overnight, distance yourself from them, and do not look for opportunities to do so either, because today they are obviously so rare that when you find them you must hold them dear and not treat them harshly. Instead you should entertain them, either offering them something special to eat or to drink and, without apology, drink with them, unless it troubles you to drink at that hour, and in doing this, you suit your actions to your words. But such methods are only appropriate for great ladies. Also, in taking wine, you should drink to someone while praising his friend, thereby pleasing him—but, my daughter, take care you make no mistake while doing this. Also, you should always have honorable women as companions, and never surround yourself with those who may be of noble birth but who are not noble of heart. You always learn something good from the virtuous, but nothing from those who are not. Also, everyone wants to be held in high regard by their families. For this reason, if God gives you children, ask Him for nothing for them except goodness and virtue, and these will be the first gifts you give them. You must carefully consider who will baptize them and instruct them in the church and who will bring them up, because whoever it is must be wise and honorable. Do not be one of those to whom it matters little who baptizes or rears their children as long as they are highly placed and noble. This is not sensible, for they may well have more faults than someone less exalted who will raise your children well. Thus you must always take great care because seeing your children poorly trained is very painful. On the other hand, there is no greater joy in the world to a father and mother than to have wise and well-taught children. Be unstinting in your efforts; teach them as well as you can, and make sure they learn as much as they can, given their limits as children. They should first learn the articles of faith, the Ten Commandments, the nature of sin, and the Seven Deadly Sins; teach them how to confess, how to conduct themselves in church and during sermons, and how they must welcome their Creator in great reverence and with humility.[73] If it so happens that one of your children wishes to enter into the religious life, praise God and do not try to discourage it, but neither should you be in a hurry to let your child undertake it if the child has neither the maturity nor the experience to make such a decision.[74] And if it does come to pass, make sure to choose a strict order, one firmly holding to a rule; to agree to any other would be foolish because of the dangers that might result. Make sure that your child will not be surrounded by those who are badly behaved so that the child will not follow a bad example, and point out the great good and honor that come from being humble and truthful. Daughters are a heavy responsibility—when they are young, you must watch over them carefully.

[27][75]

In addition, my daughter, you must ensure they are sensibly dressed, without excessive pride, so that they will not attract envy. As I told you

---

[73]   *articles of the faith* Anne's reference is to the revealed truths of Christianity. This term was not used in the early Church, but it was employed by writers with whom Anne is familiar, including Bernard of Clairvaux (n. 4, above) and Thomas Aquinas (n. 5, above); see *The Catholic Encyclopedia* [online], "articles of faith." The specific principles of Christianity, then, are to be learned, as well as the "laws" of the Old Testament, *the Ten Commandments* (Exodus 20:1–18).

   the nature of sin Sin is "a morally bad act"; see *Catholic Encyclopedia* [online], "nature of sin."

   the Seven Deadly Sins The "Seven Deadly Sins," or cardinal sins, are pride, covetousness, lust, envy, gluttony, anger, and sloth; these sins were identified and grouped together by Saint Gregory the Great, and are discussed at length by Thomas Aquinas (see *The Catholic Encyclopedia* [online], "seven deadly sins"); see also n. 47, above.

   An explanation of all these recommendations, written specifically for the laity, would have been found in *The Book of Vices and Virtues*, one of the books on Anne's reading list for Suzanne (see n. 9).

[74]   *the religious life* Anne's concern here and in the sentence that follows is for a child who might choose to become a monk or a nun, a way of religious life adhering to a "rule"; her advice to Suzanne is that, if her child expresses such a desire, she wait until the child is old enough to make such a momentous decision and that, once the decision has been made, the child be placed in a monastery or convent that follows its rule strictly—in other words, her concern is that Suzanne's child not join a lax order, becoming like the notorious Monk or worldly Prioress in Chaucer's *The Canterbury Tales*, to cite a literary example.

[75]   Chazaud inserts a section number here, a second "XXV," but in his *errata* he notes this "mistake." However, the sixteenth-century edition *does* indicate a new

before, envy will often damage their well-being and discourage their advancement; for this reason, always be sensible, setting them a good example. And when they reach an age to be fully arrayed, little by little reduce your own adornment, always conducting yourself honorably so that no one has any reason to speak ill of you; never behave as those arrogant mothers who display themselves with their daughters, next to whom they look like grandmothers! Such women are mocked, so it is better to avoid such behavior and take up some gracious pastime when you reach this age. I do not mean to say that a noblewoman, whatever her age or rank, should not, within reason, show herself to best advantage over others, but whatever beauty a woman has had, once she has passed the age of forty, there is no clothing, however beautiful, that can make the wrinkles on her face disappear. Therefore you should act your age. Do not be one of those women to whom it matters little that she conducted herself badly in her youth nor to whom it matters little how she behaves in old age; she thinks it is proper at her age to encourage the visits of a man, believing that she is loved honorably, but many bad intentions are hidden behind a "good" love. Sometimes a man deceives and abuses an envious woman, revenging himself by tricking and mocking her. Sometimes a woman is deceived for no other reason than a man's desire to spite someone *he* envies, someone who has more influence or status, but no one sees what he intends, and without the tiniest bit of love, he subtly alienates his rival and then puts himself in his place. The foolish woman is deceived by his words and believes he loves her more than she was loved before; thus she deceives herself. Her fever plunges her into the terrible heat of passion, and she is dishonored because of her own folly. At her age, the sin is greater than it was when she was young. But the sin of the man who pursued her is even worse, for, whatever his age, the beginning was bad and the end much worse.

XXVI [28]

Thus, my daughter, whatever your age, guard against being deceived and remember what I told you before because you can be blamed even for something very slight and then mocked for it, especially by idiots who create a sensation when they ridicule some woman with their snide remarks. The greater her rank, the more they think their

section begins at this point, a division that should be numbered Section 27. On this, see "Introduction," n. 58.

hot air is appreciated, and the more they talk; the larger the company, the more they say and the louder they speak because they want everyone to understand them, either by means of their words or their obvious gesturing. In the end all this is nothing but pretense and counterfeit, because no one truly noble has a heart so corrupt, and no one truly just believes such foolish disloyalty. If you wish to follow the right path, others will do nothing but mock your effort in various ways, so corrupt is the world and, in this case, so disordered—these mockers have neither reason nor conscience, and they should fear the punishment that is to come. If you want to be considered wise, you must conduct yourself wisely and chastely. Also, my daughter, wherever you are, do not behave like those foolish women who, in company, have no presence or bearing, who do not know what to say and cannot reply with even one word when someone speaks to them. They pretend to hear nothing, whether something said is to honor them or to amuse them, and when they do respond, they speak basely and rudely, which is very shameful; no noblewoman has such a nature, and if she does, she is not noble. The nature of noblewomen must be to increase their reputation for good, the better to make known their virtue, so they will be remembered for it. For this reason, my daughter, be careful and, as I have said, take the middle way and recommend it to your young women, making sure they are appropriately clothed because it is unbecoming to see young, unmarried women foolishly dressed. There must be a proper distinction between the clothing of your young attendants and that of the young women of your husband's family; your women must dress appropriately for their station. They must also conduct themselves appropriately, and not otherwise; those who behave badly sin, and are the reason why many young townswomen [put on airs]—it seems to them that they are as good as the simple ladies who are your attendants, but they cause their husbands great harm.[76] And so, my daughter, when it comes to this quality, always hold yourself and your women to the mean and the right so that your renown will be worthy of perpetual memory.

---

[76] *townswomen* Anne refers here to the *bourgeoises de ville*; the citizen of the town, or *bourg*, was the "burgher," or *bourgeois*, who occupied a social position between the peasant and the aristocrat. By the time Anne was writing her *enseignements*, some members of the *bourgeoisie* had become very wealthy; Anne's concern here is obviously for the wife of a wealthy townsman who thought herself equal to—or better than—a member of Anne's household (whom Anne refers to here as a *demoiselle*; see n. 17). From Anne's point of view, such an "upstart" woman would cause her husband problems or "harm."

XXVII [29]

Also, my daughter, if at some point in the future God takes your husband, leaving you a widow, or if your husband goes to war or into danger, leaving you alone, then you will be responsible for your children, like many other young women; have patience, because it pleases God, and govern wisely. Do not be one of those foolish women who are so frightened they rave and cry and make vows and promises they do not remember two days later, nor one of those who care so little about their honor they rush about and a month later seem no longer even to remember their dead husbands, which is very improper in a worthy woman; such women abandon their own honor and damage that of their daughters, and not without cause. For this reason, my daughter, protect yourself if such a situation arises and conduct yourself kindly and diffidently. With regard to mourning, the greatest grief is not the most praised because, as I have said before, in all things you must hold to the mean, especially when you can anger God with your excesses—but widowed women cannot offer too many prayers, fasts, or alms because devotion should be their principal occupation.[77] When it comes to the government of their lands and affairs, they must depend only on themselves; when it comes to sovereignty, they must not cede power to anyone. And, then, you must protect yourself from deceitful and presumptuous followers, especially those with whom you conduct business often, because of the suspicions that can arise; you should be just as protective of the women in your household, whether they are your attendants, relatives, or whomever. Many women are slandered by their own followers—it is a great pity when noblewomen are brought down by those who should uphold them. If you ever find yourself in such a situation, my daughter, govern wisely without getting a bad name for yourself; after serving God with great care, concern yourself with setting a good example for your children and loving them wholly and sincerely. Do not be one of those parents to whom it matters little if her children acquire any virtues as long as she see them occupying a prominent position—this is wicked and damnable, and often the children later curse their own fathers and mothers because great honor in this world is, in the end, only diversion and deception.

---

[77] *fasts* Anne's reference here is to fasting, required on certain holy days; this form of penitence or contrition could also be performed as an act of devotion, particularly as an indication of a woman's control over her physical desires.

It often happens that children so raised forget God, which their parents, in their own folly and presumption, fail to see—they are blind to it. I have seen some gentlewomen marry their daughters to knights, and these mothers then attend their own daughters, which is an act of stupidity on both their parts: arrogance in the daughter and absolute folly in the mother.[78]

XXVIII [30]

And so, my daughter, take care and always follow the mean because it is honorable and in doing so you earn God's grace and the love of those who love Him; take care to govern yourself with their counsel. If you act thus, you will give them reason to love and praise you, but if you act otherwise, they will impute it to pride and disdain and you will lose the name of nobility. Nobility is never found save in a humble, benign, and courteous heart, and every other perfection you might have—like beauty, youth, wealth, or power—is vile without the aforesaid virtues. Such lesser goods are what lead people to persist in their misunderstanding so that they fail to recognize true virtue in their families and friends and, thus, lose them—and you can never have too many. To have a multitude of family and friends, you must never be too conceited because, as the proverb goes, in prosperity you will find friends enough, but in adversity, few. In a time of need, friends will be as rare as a horse with white feet. And nothing is firm or lasting in the gifts of Fortune; today you see those raised high by Fortune who, two days later, are brought down hard.[79] You must not, therefore, trust in or be raised up by Fortune, but humble yourself and thank God, especially for those noble souls in whom every example of humility is evident and shining. Also, my daughter, do not acquire anything unjustly, and do not rejoice in what has been wrongly gained because this is damnation of the soul. In addition, do not trust in youth, strength, or beauty because we

[78] *some gentlewomen* Anne uses the phrase "some gentlewomen" (*aucunez gentilz femmes*) here, not specifying the rank of the mothers; Anne implies that, regardless of rank, for a daughter to take precedence over her mother is "an act of stupidity."

[79] *Fortune* The abstract quality of fortune is personified as "Fortune," from *Fortuna*, the Roman goddess of chance; the fickle Fortune turns her wheel, raising and lowering the unfortunate humans whose life she controls. A memorable depiction of Fortune and her wheel is found in Boethius, one of the authorities to whom Anne refers (see n. 7).

have not one certain hour, however young, strong, or beautiful we may be. And with regard to beauty, it is the most harmful and the poorest favor that God can give to one of his creatures, and the one soonest gone—with one fever it is lost. For this reason, my daughter, flee such foolish conceits because they are diabolical and they anger God: first, as I have said, for your being too arrogant and too elevated by them; second, by the gossip and hatred that results from them; and third, by your not honoring Him to whom you should give honor, which is very dishonest in a noblewoman who must, given her station, have a heart so good that she never fails to offer honor and courtesy to all every day for the great favors that God has given her. For this reason, my daughter, do not pretend to honor others because the more you do them honor, the more you increase your own. There is nothing more delightful than to see a noblewoman who recognizes virtue, which shows itself more in those who are noble than in others. But it is not enough to open your mouth and mutter a greeting; you must welcome everyone with the kind word and nod of your head that is appropriate to their rank, and make an effort to remember what is due them. Also, you must do this for everyone, whether arriving or departing, because these are the obligations of nobility. To acquire a good reputation and a great number of friends you must be moved by humility, believing that those who are greatest have greatest need of it. Therefore, my daughter, take care, and you will be greatly praised for it. A wise person does not fail to pursue such virtues in youth; for this reason, I counsel you to fix them in your heart so that they will always serve you and be your rule in life, without your having to learn them when you should already know them, although it is not a disgrace to be learning always. For this reason you should associate with those who are wise—to learn and then to remember good teachings and doctrines. Do not be one of those arrogant and foolish women who, when someone reproves her gently or instructs her kindly, becomes annoyed and takes it badly. In her arrogance, she thinks she is wiser and more knowledgeable and thus drowns in her own opinions. As it is commonly said, you are not a fool unless you think you are wise. And those who are young think they have seen and understood more than anyone else even though it is impossible for those who are oldest not to have seen more. Also, one of the greatest signs of love that you can show others is to correct their faults sweetly. For this reason, my daughter, if God gives you friends who remonstrate with you, thank them with a good heart and take care to put into effect what they have taught you, without relying on your own judgment.

XXIX [31]

Finally, my daughter, as good counsel and as a general rule, make sure that all your desires, works, wants, and wishes are in God and to His credit, meanwhile awaiting His grace and just dispositions in great humility of heart; have firm faith and hope in Him, recommending your soul and all your affairs to Him. Recommend yourself as well to the sweet Virgin Mary, praying that she will, out of grace, want to be your advocate with her dear Son; pray also that you are able to live without reproach in this world, that you can preserve your honor in all purity and cleanness.[80] It is a precious treasure which much be carefully preserved. Honor is noble and excellent when it is wholly preserved; once even slightly overcome or damaged, you can never find a way to restore its worth. For this reason, my daughter, for fear that you will be deceived, you cannot guard your honor too carefully. And if it happens that someone makes a request that troubles you, do not be ashamed but, graciously, make your excuses to the man who makes it, whether he is great or small, and always use kind and humble words because the more you are valued for your honor, the less will be requested of your dishonor. Know that when you make proud responses, he will ask more of you because he will think this vice is not your only one and that, in the end, you will not be so vexed after all—and he will soon gain his desired goal; so, then, make sure to be kind in all things.

XXX [32]

And so, my daughter, if this situation arises, conduct yourself wisely, as women of rank should, and commend yourself with a good heart to the Virgin Mary, and she will succor you in all your necessities and affairs. Always bear yourself honorably, with a cool and assured manner, a humble gaze, and a quiet word; be constant and firm every day, to each proposal, without bending. And concerning your excuses to those who make unreasonable requests of you, you should say that you cannot believe that their hearts are so debased that they could put them to such vile things, and then show them the eternal joys and

[80] *purity and cleanness* Anne's concern here and in Section XXX [32] is that Suzanne preserve her chastity, her "honor," which becomes more clear as this section develops.

honorable praise that is to be acquired by the excellent virtue of chastity, without contradicting what you have said by any promises or words. And, above all, you must fly the acquaintance of such men because it is the best way to protect yourself. I do not wish to say that you will never encounter them even in good company, or that in hearing, speaking, and responding to honest questions and proposals you might not sometimes encounter the bad as well as the good. But, suppose a castle is beautiful and so well-guarded that it is never assailed—then it is not to be praised, nor is a knight who has never proven himself to be commended for his prowess. To the contrary, the thing most highly commended is that which has been in the fire yet cannot be scorched (or worse) or that which has been in the terrible depths of the sea yet cannot be drowned or that which has been in the mire of this world yet cannot be soiled in any way. Worthy of being praised, therefore, are women who in this miserable world know to live in purity of conscience and chastity; they are worthy of eternal glory because by their steadfast chastity and good virtue they redirect fools, disordered in their carnality, to the good road. As the saying goes, the habit does not make the monk, and sometimes those you think are the biggest deceivers and the most worldly are easiest to convert and greatly to be commended. Nevertheless, in this situation there is no certainty, and I counsel more doubt than surety. As Saint Paul says, the assaults and stings of this world are hard to endure except with the help of God, with which nothing is impossible.

XXXI [33]

And so, my daughter, to come to the conclusion of our discussion, to acquire the highest glory and the greatest grace in this world, to draw yourself to devotion, and to protect yourself from the temptations that will come to you for the aforesaid reasons (like delicious food, gaieties of heart, or other things), reflect carefully that, in the end, you must die. For this reason, take great care to live well so that you have no reason to doubt the end, and so that you have the grace of God in this world and in the next: His glory, which the Father, the Son, and the Holy Spirit bestow on you.

Interpretive Essay

The Princess and *The Prince*: gender, genre, and *Lessons for My Daughter*

Without the authority guaranteed by the title of regent, Anne of France nevertheless managed to wield her considerable power quite effectively during the years she governed France, but just *how* she managed to do so was not at all clear to her contemporaries, nor is it any more clear to us today. As her supporters and detractors struggled to explain the role she assumed after her father's death, they had a great deal to say about her, but very little of what they said offered any analysis of her decisions or any insight into the political philosophy driving those decisions. Nor do her own words clarify the obscurity; only a handful of her letters survive, and they reveal neither motive nor method and only, on rare occasion, the merest of personal details.[1] But the lack of information seems deliberate rather than accidental. Perhaps the most astute assessment of Anne of France's methods remains that of the nineteenth-century historian Jules Michelet: "It seems . . . that she took as much care to conceal her power as others do to show theirs."[2]

Given their inability to penetrate her opacity, her contemporaries were left at times stating the obvious. "Madame Anne de

---

[1] In his portrait of Anne of France, Pierre de Bourdeille, abbé of Brantôme (c. 1540–1614) wrote, "I have read many letters from her to our family in the days of her greatness," a claim that has generally been used by historians and biographers to conclude that a voluminous correspondence has been lost; see his *Vies des dames illustres*, published as *Illustrious Dames of the Court of Valois Kings*, trans. Katharine Prescott Wormeley (New York: Lamb Publishing, 1912), 218. (For Brantôme's relationship to Anne of France, see "Introduction," 6.)

All those who write about Anne of France in any detail remark on the loss of her letters—see, most recently, Pauline Matarasso, *Queen's Mate: Three Women of Power in France on the Eve of the Renaissance* (Burlington, VT: Ashgate, 2001), 45. Matarasso has collected, translated, and published the greatest number of Anne's letters in one place to date. One of her calculations is very revealing: in analyzing the correspondence to and from Charles VIII in the spring and summer of 1488 (a period of 170 days), she notes the survival of 118 letters dictated by Charles, 16 from Pierre of Beaujeu, and only 5 from Anne (p. 44).

[2] Jules Michelet, *Histoire de France*, quoted in Jean-Marie de la Mure, *Histoire des ducs de Bourbon et des comtes de Forez . . .* , ed. R. Chantelauze (Paris: A. Montbrison, 1868), 2:327 n.

France . . . governed the person of the king," one chronicler noted, while another remarked that she not only controlled the king but "all the realm"; "Madam Beaujeu . . . controlled the throne of France," still another confirmed, adding that "the said lady . . . dispatched all the difficult business of the realm."[3] Still, there was more than just acknowledgment of her power; according to one observer, the great men of the realm were also "indignant."[4] She might be "sage, prudent, and virtuous," or "one of the most beautiful and honest ladies that was ever known, and . . . [one] of the most wise and virtuous," but she was still a woman, and "many were very unhappy that Anne, the sister of Charles, was preferred over others in matters of government."[5] In trying to explain Anne of France, her contemporaries thus came to focus on her sex rather than her abilities.

Unable to see in her the kind of woman they expected, they saw her, instead, as a woman who possessed the abilities of a man. She was, in the words of one chronicler, a "*virago*, truly superior to her sex," a woman who was both "skilled and fearless" and who "ceded neither resolution nor courage to men."[6] She was thus a "perfect model" in all respects save one: she was a woman. The writer indicated the difficulty of Anne's position, if not the tragedy. She had surely been "born to the glory of royal sovereignty" except for the unfortunate fact that "nature" had "deprived" her of "that sex"—"*that* sex" being the male sex, necessary for kingship.

As a woman who had the abilities deemed appropriate only for a man, Anne was often compared *to* men, most obviously her father. "One finds in her much of the spirit and character of Louis XI," wrote a contemporary.[7] Another judged her to be "haughty, unrelenting, guided in all she did by her father's maxims and just like him in character."[8] She was "a shrewd woman and a cunning if ever there was

---

[3]   Jean Bouchet, Olivier de la Marche, and Alain Bouchart, quoted by John S. C. Bridge, *A History of France from the Death of Louis XI*, vol. 1: *Reign of Charles VIII, Regency of Anne of Beaujeu, 1483–1493* (1921; rpt. New York, Octagon Books, 1978), 51–52.

[4]   Jean de Bourdigné, quoted by Bridge, 1:52.

[5]   Nicole Gilles, quoted by Bridge, 1:52 n; Claude de Seyssel, quoted in de la Mure, 2:327 n; Pierre Desrey, quoted by Bridge, 1:52 n.

[6]   The Latin chronicle, incorporated into Guillaume de Jaligny's history of Charles VIII, is quoted in de la Mure, 2:326 n. and 344 n. The chronicler uses the Latin *virago*, which can mean "man-like woman," "woman warrior," or "heroic maiden"; see, for example, the *Chambers Murray Latin-English Dictionary* and the *Oxford English Dictionary*.

[7]   Quoted in de la Mure, 2:326 n.

[8]   Quoted by Matarasso, 12.

one," wrote Brantôme at the outset of his portrait of Anne of France, "the true image of King Louis, her father." "The choice made of her to be guardian and administrator of her brother . . . proves this," he claimed, and as support he offered that she was "very vindictive in temper like her father, and always a sly dissembler, corrupt, full of deceit, and a great hypocrite, who, for the sake of her ambition, could mask and disguise herself in any way." Though she "governed" her brother "so wisely and virtuously that he came to be one of the greatest of the kings of France," and although she was also "wise and virtuous" in her rule of the kingdom, Brantôme just could not bring himself to approve of her; she "held to her grandeur terribly," addressed others "bravely" but "imperiously" (even more bravely and imperiously than "any" of the kings he had known, adding, lest we should doubt him, "and I have seen many"), and was "a *maîtresse femme*, though quarrelsome." His final comment perfectly demonstrates his ambivalence: "To end all, this Anne de France was very clever and sufficiently good. I have now said enough about her."[9] As Pauline Matarasso notes, it is still "tempting" even now for us to see her as "very much her father's child," because "Louis is so much easier to know," a "self-confessed babbler" who left behind a "voluminous correspondence.[10] But, while Anne's contemporaries saw in her a woman deprived of "that sex" more appropriate to her abilities, her father—despite his generally poor view of women—saw the female in himself, engaging in a bit of gender analysis of his own. "I am like a woman," he once wrote, "when anyone tells me anything in an obscure manner I must know at once what it is all about."[11]

When not appreciated or condemned for the qualities she shared with her father, she was compared to her husband, the comparisons showing how the couple and their partnership challenged conceptions of sex and gender. Never one of Anne's admirers, Claude de Seyssel described her husband as "a peaceful, kind man of good will, without malice or trickery"—but one who served his "redoubtable wife" with a kind of blind devotion.[12] Another contemporary described Pierre of Bourbon as intelligent and experienced, but "with a character in which gentleness and complaisance were pushed to the point of

---

[9] Brantôme, 216–18.
[10] Matarasso, 12.
[11] Quoted by Matarasso, 12.
[12] One of Louis XII's counselors, Claude de Seyssel (1450-c. 1520) wrote a panegyric of the king he served, *Histoire singulière de Louis XII*; quoted in de la Mure, 2:327 n.

feebleness"; he was "good and easygoing and very different than his rigorous wife," another noted, adding that Anne was "the master," using her "authority as the daughter of the king" to control her husband.[13] The word *douceur*—meaning mildness, gentleness, or softness—is frequently used to described Pierre, but not his wife.[14] About the relationship between the two, Brantôme was deliciously spiteful: "It is true . . . that she made him do what she had in her head, for she ruled him and knew how to guide him, all the better because he was rather foolish—indeed very much so. . . ."[15]

Her relationship with her brother also became an issue. It was traditional, even expected, for a mother to act as regent for her son— one recent analysis of the regency as it developed in France has described it as something of a "vocation" for royal women—but Louis XI ignored whatever expectations Charlotte of Savoy might have had when he designated his daughter to fulfill the *role* of regent without having the authority guaranteed by the *title*.[16] Anne's supporters initially used her relationship to the young king to her advantage; as the king's sister, she could be relied on to guide, nurture, and defend her brother, not to challenge him or to usurp his crown. The young king had been raised "courteously and honestly," but was still in need of being "nourished and protected with great solicitude and diligence," and thus the Estates General, convened by Anne early in 1484, concluded that Charles should remain in his sister's care.[17]

But once the young king was placed in his sister's hands, her control of him became an issue. Guillaume de Jaligny, the Beaujeus' secretary, wrote that "Madam" was always with the king and that nothing concerning him or the country was decided without her knowledge,

---

[13] Contemporary assessments quoted by Bridge, 1:33–34 and Marc Chombart de Lauwe, *Anne de Beaujeu: ou la passion du pouvoir* (Paris: Librairie Jules Tallandier, 1980), 397 n.

[14] See, for example, the descriptions quoted by de la Mure, 2:327 n.

[15] Brantôme, 217.

[16] On possible motivations for Louis XI, see "Appendix I," 91.

For the role of regent as "vocation," see André Poulet, "Capetian Women and the Regency: The Genesis of a Vocation," in John Carmi Parsons, ed., *Medieval Queenship* (New York: St. Martin's Press, 1993), 93–116, and Sharon L. Jansen, *The Monstrous Regiment of Women: Female Rulers in Early Modern Europe* (New York: Palgrave Macmillan, 2002), 57–60 and 247–49. See also Marion F. Facinger, "A Study of Medieval Queenship: Capetian France, 987–1237," *Studies in Medieval and Renaissance History* 5 (1968), 3–47 and Fanny Cosandey, "De lance en quenouille. La place de la reine dans l'État moderne (14ᵉ –17ᵉ siècles)," *Annales* 53 (1997), 799–820.

[17] Council decision of 10 February 1484 quoted in de la Mure, 2:334 n.

contrary to her desires, or lacking her consent.[18] Diplomats to France and ambassadors within the country also carried or sent similar assessments to their respective governments; the Venetian ambassador, for example, noted that Anne's agreement was needed for any proposal, while a Spanish diplomat simply delivered proposals sent by Isabella of Castile directly to Anne of France.[19] Such control was resented. Her opponents "claimed that the King was kept in subjection and his authority was usurped," laying "the whole blame upon Anne"; what seemed particularly galling was that she was a woman and "barely" twenty years old.[20] In his memoirs, Philippe de Commynes claimed that Charles treated his sister with "a fearful deference," while Seyssel suggested that Anne's ability to control her brother was only to be expected because Charles had been "reared among women, with few men about him and those mediocre."[21]

The duke of Orléans, heir presumptive to the throne, was quick to use Anne's challenge to established gender roles to his advantage. At the banquet following her brother's coronation, Anne's surveillance and the king's reaction were observed; "Madam de Beaujeu came through the Chapel door, and entered the hall, to see how the King was behaving himself," one of these observers noted. Charles was said to have fallen immediately silent; seeing this, Orléans commented, "Madame de Beaujeu, your sister . . . wants to keep you in leading-strings and to have rule over you and your kingdom."[22] In the same vein, Francis II of Brittany rallied support for Orléans during the Mad War by denouncing the "subjection" in which the French king was held "*by a woman.*"[23] Pierre Landois, on trial for his role in the Orléans rebellion, blamed—or explained—his participation on his "fear of the said lady and her adherents, who want to control everything and govern everyone."[24] Brantôme also regarded Louis of Orléans as motivated, at least in part, by sexual politics. He interpreted Anne's control of the government as a kind of jealous revenge, motivated by "the

---

[18] Bridge, 1:50 n.

[19] Bridge, 1:51 n.

[20] Quoted by Bridge, 1:50 n.

[21] Philippe de Commynes (1447–1511), whose *Mémoires* are quoted in de la Mure, 2:326 n; Claude de Seyssel is quoted by Matarasso, 75.

[22] Bridge, 1:31. The duke seems to have used this "gender card" effectively, since, as Matarasso notes, Charles and Orléans were "inseparable through the summer months" (24).

[23] The duke of Brittany's letter is quoted by Bridge, 1:50 n; the italics are mine. For the Mad War, see "Introduction," n. 24.

[24] Quoted by Bridge, 1:50 n.

hatred she bore to M. d' Orléans" who had spurned her love; "in the beginning," according to Brantôme, Anne "loved him with love." But Louis was unwilling "to hear her" because he wanted a wife who would "depend upon him as first and nearest prince to the crown, and not upon herself." Anne could not accept her rightful place as a woman: "she desired the contrary, for she wanted to hold the highest place and to govern in all things." Louis "might have had better luck" if only he had been able to "constrain himself," but he "could not," seeing her "so ambitious."[25] It is ironic, then, that when Louis of Orléans became king after Charles VIII's death and married the widowed Anne of Brittany, he was judged to be "weak, submitting to the disastrous influence of his wife, whom he did not know how to resist and about whom he said, to excuse himself, that it was necessary 'to suffer some things for a wife, when she loves her husband and her honor.' "[26]

Such is not only the context in which Anne of France lived and maneuvered, it is also the context in which she wrote her lessons for her daughter, and thus to raise questions about gender in Anne of France's *Lessons* is not to distort her text by reading a fifteenth-century work from a twenty-first century perspective. Sex and gender were central to the discussion of her role from the beginning. But we should also note that such conflicted and conflicting views of sex, gender, and power persist and are also the context in which we—as readers, historians, and critics—still live and maneuver. Such views often color our interpretations of Anne of France, her political decisions, and, ultimately, her lessons to her daughter.

Even Anne's most sympathetic readers have at times regarded her with outrage and condemnation, and such judgments can certainly be sustained; like all those in power, she could at times act in ways that even her most ardent admirers condemn. But their responses seem to reflect not so much what Anne did while she was a political agent as how she ought to have acted—as a woman—regardless of the political realities. For example, she did nothing when Louis XII, who had been forced to marry her younger sister Jeanne, divorced her after he became king.[27] Even while recognizing the political necessities

---

[25]   Brantôme, 217.

[26]   de Lauwe, 423.

[27]   Born in 1464, Jeanne was betrothed to Louis of Orléans when she was three weeks old and he was two. Since Louis XI had two daughters but, as yet, no son, the proposed marriage of his younger daughter to the heir presumptive to the throne was perfectly understandable (when Orléans himself became king, he married his daughter Claude to the heir-presumptive, Francis of Angoulême).

and acknowledging that any intervention would have been fruitless, her modern biographers have nevertheless concluded that Anne's inaction proves she "had no heart"; her silence is "abominable" and "dreadful."[28] And she also accepted benefits from the new king, thus "profiting" from her sister's humiliation and demonstrating her corruption, her lack of scruples, and a singularly unfeminine "weakness," her willingness to sacrifice anyone and anything for money.[29] Loving "power for the sake of power," she was not "troubled by conscience"; though she was "beautiful," she lacked "tenderness, generosity," and "perhaps even femininity."[30] Even her most careful and sensitive reader to date concludes that the lessons she composed for her daughter "are singularly lacking in love, almost shockingly so when one considers that they were compiled by a mother for her only child," arriving at such a conclusion apparently because there are "no expressions of affection" in the *enseignements* she composed.[31]

Jeanne's physical disabilities did not prevent her father from compelling Orléans to marry her in 1476; the king reportedly forced his son-in-law to consummate the marriage as well so that there could be no grounds for annulment.

By the terms of Charles VIII and Anne of Brittany's marriage contract, if the French king predeceased his queen, she was to marry his successor. The Breton marriage had followed the Mad War and ended its follies, its purpose to end the independence of Brittany and to annex the duchy permanently to France. When Orléans became king, that purpose remained intact. Also crucial was the French succession; the twenty-two year marriage between Louis and Jeanne was childless.

28 de Lauwe devotes an entire chapter of his biography of Anne of France to *la reine sacrifiée*; the assessment that Anne had no heart is quoted on p. 398, the "abominable silence" comes from p. 365. The assessment that her silence was "dreadful" comes from Pierre Pradel, *Anne de France, 1461–1522* (Paris: Editions Publisud, 1986), 161. Here Jehanne d'Orliac, though writing much earlier, notes the political necessity of the divorce and of Anne's "neutrality," even while admitting the pain for all concerned; see *Anne de Beaujeu: roi de France* (Paris: Librairie Plon, 1926), 145–47. Bridge's assessment is that the divorce was a "necessity as imperious as any that ever dictated the conduct of a ruler"; he also cites papal historian Mandell Creighton, who judged that "if ever the dissolution could be justified on grounds of political expediency, the justification might be urged in this case" (3:18).

29 de Lauwe, 455; Pradel, 161. But see d'Orliac, 151, who questions whether the "material advantages" Anne received are evidence of avarice (148–49). About the charge of rapacity, Bridge concludes, "the striking thing is, not that she took what she did, but that she took so little" (1:246).

30 de Lauwe, 455–56.

31 Matarasso, 194, but see "Appendix II," 95. Matarasso otherwise avoids the pitfalls of de Lauwe and Pradel; about the divorce, for example, which she treats in a chapter entitled "A Sorry Business," she concludes that although "[o]ne might

As adroit—and experienced—a politician as Anne of France was doubtless well aware of the way she was viewed by her contemporaries, and rather than making a show of her power and control, she preferred to remain behind the scenes.[32] When first establishing her position, for example, she did nothing in her own name; she acted "in guardianship" of her brother and "in obedience" to her husband; when faced with the opposition of Louis of Orléans, she attempted first to "seduce" him rather than to "reduce" him, organizing banquets and processions, offering concessions, conciliations, and rewards, and naming Louis lieutenant general of Paris.[33] She preferred "adroit flattery" and deception to displays of power.[34] Having managed to steer her own course so successfully for so long, she was able to offer her daughter advice intended to help her negotiate the difficult passage of a "feminine and weak creature" in the world of politics.

The reading of Anne's *Lessons* offered here is not one that has been widely considered. Her text has generally been read as a conduct book, an example of that genre of didactic literature generally written by men with the aim of controlling women's behavior; in this view, Anne's is a derivative work, notable primarily for its royal (and female) author or for her familiarity with Christine de Pizan.[35] Rarely has Anne's work been considered to have any political

have hoped that Jeanne . . . would have received support from her sister," Anne saw the "imperatives" the new king faced and "bowed with her usual cool grace to the inevitable" (155).

[32] As we have seen, she remained behind the scenes during the banquet following her brother's coronation; as another example, when the Estates convened in January 1484, the fifteen-year-old Charles was seated on the throne while Anne herself did not appear.

[33] For this assessment of Anne's strategy and methods, see d'Orliac, 65–76.

[34] de la Mure, 2:330 n.

[35] For this reading of Anne of France's *Lessons,* see Alice A. Hentsch, *De la Littérature didactique du moyen age, s'adressant spécialement aux femmes* (Cahors, France: A. Coueslant, 1903); Colette H. Winn, " '*De mères en filles*': Les manuels d'éducation sous l'Ancien Régime," *Atlantis 19.1* (1983), 23–29; Charity Cannon Willard, "Anne de France, Reader of Christine de Pizan" in Glenda K. McLeod, ed., *The Reception of Christine de Pizan from the Fifteenth through the Nineteenth Centuries: Visitors to the City* (Lewiston, NY: Edwin Mellen Press, 1991), 59–69; Colette H. Winn, "*La Dignitas Mulieris*: Les Enjeux idéologiques d'une appropriation du xve au xviie siècle," *Études Littéraires* 27.2 (1994), 11–24; and Roberta L. Krueger, "*Chascune selon son estat*: Women's Education and Social Class in the Conduct Books of Christine de Pizan and Anne de France," *Papers on French Seventeenth Century Literature* 24.46 (1997), 19–34.

On conduct books for women, see Diane Bornstein, *The Lady in the Tower: Medieval Courtesy Literature for Women* (Hamden: Archon Books, 1983);

relevance, and when the question has been raised, it has been dismissed. In her reading of Anne of France's *enseignements*, for example, Constance Jordan argues that, by advising her daughter to "take account of her feminine weakness and, as a rule, to *decline* to use whatever authority or power she may have," Anne's instructions are aimed at diminishing, rather than fostering, a woman's abilities. In "mask[ing] her knowledge of court affairs," and in "avoid[ing] above all the impression of *being in command*," a woman will lose power: "she cannot function politically," Jordan writes. "These warnings," she concludes, "seem to come from the author's personal experience of court politics; certainly they convey a sense of her own isolation and her fear that her presence at court would elicit envy rather than awe and loyalty."[36] In the most extensive analysis of the *Lessons* to date, Pauline Matarasso comes to similar conclusions. "If Anne had followed the precepts she professes in her maturity she would never have ruled a nation in her youth," she writes: "This woman of power who has held in her hand lines of communication running from Brest to Constantinople, from the Baltic to the Mediterranean, whose *fiat* has moved armies and whose counsel in later years was sought by princes and their envoys, has nothing to say to her daughter on any issues other than domestic."[37]

I am not inclined to dismiss Anne's *enseignements* so completely, however, for it seems to me that her book of instruction is as subtle as *Madame la Grande* herself. Her *Lessons* carefully prepare Suzanne to act *both* circumspectly *and* politically. In drawing her portrait of an ideal princess, Anne presents a guidebook on governance for Suzanne, one not altogether unlike Machiavelli's more famous book of advice for a would-be prince, written some fifteen years later. In addressing

Evelyne Berriot Salvador, "Les Femmes et les pratiques de l'écriture de Christine de Pisan à Marie de Gournay," *Reforme, Humanisme, Renaissance* 9.16 (1983), 52–69; Kathleen Ashley, "Medieval Courtesy Literature and Dramatic Mirrors of Female Conduct" in *The Ideology of Conduct*, ed. Nancy Armstrong and Leonard Tennenhouse (New York: Methuen, 1987), 25–38; Felicity Riddy, "Mother Knows Best: Reading Social Change in a Courtesy Text," *Speculum* 71.1 (1996), 66–86; and Susan Udry, "Books of Women's Conduct from France during the High and Late Middle Ages, 1200–1400," ORB Online Encyclopedia; available from http://the-orb.net/encyclop/culture/women/books4women.htm; accessed 9 May 2003. Udry notes, "Although there were conduct books written for men, the greater number of surviving manuscripts . . . is directed toward the supervision and control of women's activity in domestic settings."

[36] *Renaissance Feminism: Literary Texts and Political Models* (Ithaca, NY: Cornell University Press, 1990), 97–98.

[37] Matarasso, 13, 194.

The Prince to Lorenzo de' Medici, Machiavelli hoped that his "understanding of the deeds of great men, acquired through a lengthy experience of contemporary politics and through an uninterrupted study of the classics" would prove useful to the new ruler; the book thus represented "everything" he had "learned over the course of so many years, and [had] undergone so many discomforts and dangers to discover." As such, he could offer "no greater gift"—there is nothing among his possessions he values "more," and nothing he "would put a higher price upon."[38] So the *enseignements* from Anne of France to her daughter.

Such a comparison is not as improbable as it may sound, for Anne of France's political pragmatism has been widely recognized. She adjusted her principles to her circumstances and her interests: "Divide in order to rule; separate your enemies in order to overcome them more easily; use any means necessary as long as they are used skillfully; take back with one hand what you have given with the other."[39] She well knew the ruses, evasions, and disguises needed "not only to be great, but merely to live with dignity."[40] "He who knows how to conceal knows how to rule," her father once wrote.[41] Anne knew how to conceal. She "possessed the qualities and the faults of an unscrupulous man of affairs," and she knew how to "play the game of intrigue."[42] Even while dismissing a political reading of the *Lessons*, Matarasso connects Anne of France with Machiavelli explicitly: "In government a Machiavellian pragmatism had guided her decisions."[43] And thus I would argue that assumptions about gender and genre have not only shaped her contemporaries' "reading" of Anne of France, but have also shaped our contemporaries' reading of her *Lessons*.

Before examining this comparison in more detail, I would like to recall the models Anne of France turned to when she composed her work. It was her nineteenth century editor who noted the "obligatory" and "familial" nature of her task, pointing to Louis IX's *enseignements* and her father's *The Rosetree of Wars* as her models when she composed her *Lessons*; in preparing her advice for

---

[38] "Niccolò Machiavelli to His Magnificence Lorenzo de' Medici," *The Prince*, ed. and trans. David Wootton (Indianapolis, IN: Hackett Publishing, 1995), 5.

[39] Pélicier, 212 and 206; Pélicier calls these the "lessons" that Louis XI "passed on" to his daughter.

[40] d'Orliac, 172.

[41] Hedwige de Chabannes and Isabelle de Linarès, *Anne de Beaujeu: "Ce fut ung roy"* (Paris: Crépin-Leblond, 1955), 17.

[42] de Lauwe, 455; Pradel, 181.

[43] Matarasso, 289.

Suzanne, she was assuming a responsibility for carrying on this "paternal work."[44] As we have seen, Louis IX had prepared two separate sets of instructions, one for a son, who would succeed his father as king, and a second for a daughter, who would be a queen consort but not a queen regnant. Anne seems deliberately to have shaped her lessons to recall these *enseignements* offered to a "dear son" and a "dear daughter."[45] In her own words, she is merely a mother offering "a few little lessons" to her own daughter, whom she addresses directly (*ma fille*) throughout, just as Louis IX had directly addressed his "dear daughter" Isabelle, but at the same time she is also compiling a list exactly like the one the king had offered to his son. And while constructing a work that *seems* to be appropriate in its form and address, a series of lessons that could be addressed to a daughter as well as a son, she is at the same time creating one that could be read very differently. In its openness to the possibility of multiple readings, her *Lessons* must also be compared to her father's lessons which can be read in very different ways: the reader will see what the reader expects to see. As Louis XI's biographer reads *The Rosetree of Wars*, the work "may be ranked with the King's letters, his instructions to ambassadors and the preambles to his laws as reflecting more clearly than any other document the mind of the King, his earnest desire for peace and for the public good, and his conviction that experience is the best method of instruction."[46] But as F. Leclercq suggests, the work can also be read quite differently. "*The Rosetree of Wars* should be appreciated for what it is and at the same time for what it is not but pretends to be," he writes; it is a "decent account" of the "indecencies" of political necessity, a first glance into a world of political reality that would be more fully revealed by Machiavelli.[47] In composing her *Lessons*, Anne of France has followed the model provided by her father; she has shaped a text that conforms to expectations even while it suggests how to subvert them. She might just as well have entitled her own work *The Rosetree of Wars*, the "wars" in this case the very particular

---

[44]   A.-M. Chazaud, *Les Enseignements d'Anne de France . . . à sa fille Susanne de Bourbon* (Moulins: C. Desrosiers, 1878), xv–xix. For her use of these models, as opposed to those offered by contemporary conduct books, see "Introduction," 12–16.

[45]   On Louis IX's *enseignements*, see "Introduction," 14–15.

[46]   Pierre Champion, *Louis XI*, trans. Winifred Stephens Whale (New York: Dodd, Mead & Company, 1929), 20. See also Paul Murray Kendall, *Louis XI* (New York: W. W. Norton, 1971).

[47]   "Preface," *Louis XI: Le Rozier des guerres* (Paris: L'Insomniaque, 1994), vii–ix.

set of conflicts that the young Suzanne will face; these are battles she can only win if she does not appear to fight them.[48]

And it is also important to note before proceeding further that *The Prince*, arguably the most well-known and influential work of Renaissance political theory, offers by implication acceptance of, if not support for, women rulers. Among all of the questions Machiavelli raises—should a ruler be generous? should a ruler always keep his word? is it better for a ruler to be loved or feared?—he never asks the question, "can a woman govern?" Instead, Machiavelli accepts the idea of a female ruler. In his discussion of mercenary soldiers, for example, he notes that they failed Joanna II of Naples. In listing the rulers who met the invading Louis XII of France and "sought his friendship," he includes without comment, "the Countess of Forlì," Caterina Sforza, who controlled the strategically placed cities of Imola and Forlì as regent for her son. In his assessment of the value of fortresses, he notes that there is no evidence of their usefulness to rulers, with the exception of Caterina Sforza, who successfully used Ravaldino as a refuge after her husband's assassination until she could gain control of the city. In commenting on Caterina's ultimate defeat by Cesare Borgia, he attributes her loss not to her sex—or even to some weakness in her fortress—but to a ruler's failure to avoid the hatred of the people. Machiavelli does not seem to regard sex as an issue for "the prince." He accepts, without comment, the fact of rule by women.[49]

Like Machiavelli, Anne of France accepts what is. There is simply no point in advising her daughter to defy traditional views of what it means to be a "feminine and weak creature" or to resist conventional expectations of her as a woman; rather, she seems to accept that the way for a woman to operate effectively as a ruler is to take into account her "female nature" and to use it to her purpose. In such a way she will be in command even as she cultivates the appearance of *not* being in command. It is of course "praiseworthy," as Machiavelli writes, for a ruler to live "without relying on craftiness." But "in these days" a would-be prince must know how "to employ cunning to confuse and

---

[48] I find it very intriguing that *The Rosetree of Wars* first appeared in print in 1521, the year generally suggested for the publication of Anne's *enseignements*. Is this simultaneous publication a coincidence?

[49] For Machiavelli's references to Joanna II, queen regnant of Naples (1371–1435), see *The Prince*, 39–40. For the references to Anne of France's contemporary, Caterina Sforza (1462–1509), regent of Imola and Forlì, see pp. 12 and 67; the countess of Forlì is also mentioned in his *Discourses on Livy*—see the edition of Harvey C. Mansfield and Nathan Tarcov (Chicago, 1996), XIII.6.18. (Machiavelli's first diplomatic assignment was to Caterina Sforza; see Jansen, 38–53.)

disorient other men"; such a prince will achieve "great things."[50] Just
so Anne advises her daughter: "you should have eyes to notice everything yet to see nothing, ears to hear everything yet to know nothing,
and a tongue to answer everyone yet to say nothing prejudicial to anyone." As Machiavelli would later argue, a prince is judged by what he
seems to be, not necessarily what he is: he "must seem" to be "pious,
truthful, reliable, sympathetic, and religious" to all of those "who listen to him and watch him." "Everyone sees what you seem to be," he
notes, but "few have direct experience of who you really are."[51] For
Suzanne of Bourbon, "everyone" will see what she "seems" to be, a
"feminine and weak creature," not necessarily what she is. As readers
we must neither dismiss Anne of France's insights too quickly nor
ignore the realities of the situation within which such a woman must
make her way. What we recognize as shrewdness in advice to a prince
should not be identified as weakness when it is offered to a princess.[52]

Throughout his study of the "practical realities" in which the prince
must operate, Machiavelli focuses on the quality of *virtù*, or virtue,
identified with manliness, as the word's origin, *vir*, suggests. But *virtù*,
as Machiavelli defines it, encompasses neither the Christian virtues
of faith, hope, and love, nor the classical "manly" virtues of courage,
prudence, temperance, and justice.[53] Rather, Machiavelli advocates

---

[50] *The Prince*, 48, 53.

[51] *The Prince*, 55.

[52] Such a recognition is also important when examining Christine de Pizan's advice
to "the princess" in *The Treasure*. The "fourth teaching of Prudence," about the
calculated use of a "discreet manner," admits that no one is loved by everyone.
Thus she provides the princess with a "remedy"; rather than recognizing the
affronts of those who wish to harm her, she advises that "by being friendly to them
she will make them think that she regards them highly as her friends and would
never believe that they might be otherwise. They will think that she has more trust
in them than anyone else. But she should be so wise and circumspect that no one
can perceive that she does it calculatingly . . . ." But she must avoid seeming insin-
cere or inconsistent: "The sensible thing is to observe moderation in this matter,
and it is indeed necessary to be prepared for the situation before it arises. She will
pretend that she wishes to defer to them and their advice, and she will summon
them to confidential meetings (as she will pretend them to be), where she will tell
them ordinary things with a great show of secrecy and confidence and keep her
real thoughts to herself. It is best to do this with the appearance of sincerity so that
it does not put them on their guard" (Sarah Lawson, trans., *Christine de Pisan: The
Treasure of the City of Ladies, or the Book of the Three Virtues* [New York: Penguin
Books, 1985], 69).

[53] About Machiavelli's concept of *virtù*, Wootton concludes, "The virtuous man is
the man who has those qualities that lead to success in his chosen activity"
(xxix). On these moral virtues, see "Introduction," 19 and n. 62.

those "virtues" necessary for survival and success—concealment, deception, and manipulation, not usually considered virtues, manly or otherwise. Such qualities are, in fact, the vices which were stereotypically associated with women and their wiles. Like Machiavelli, Anne of France is also concerned for the practical realities of the world Suzanne must inhabit, and she, too, is concerned with virtue: "all women who wish to have a good reputation and be recognized as worthy should have their hearts, their wills, and their minds so wholly raised on high that their principal aim is always focused on the acquisition of virtue," she writes. And, in particular, this should be a goal not just for "all women" but for Suzanne herself; "devote yourself completely to acquiring virtue," her mother urges. Unlike Machiavelli, she *is* concerned with Christian virtues, and especially with feminine virtue, with humility, patience, obedience, and complaisance, for example. But above all she stresses chastity.

It is easy to see in this emphasis on chastity both religious and cultural imperatives for women, but it is something more as well, for one of the most frequent means to discredit a woman who exerted political power was to accuse her of sexual impropriety or promiscuity. Such allegations linked a woman's sexual and political "transgressions"; her disorderly sexuality suggested her political ambitions were similarly out of order. For women the personal was always political. Thus Isabel of Bavaria had been attacked, and her regency discredited; so, too, Margaret of Anjou's effort to preserve the English crown for her son were undermined by propaganda accusing her of adultery and naming her son a bastard.[54] But no such charge was ever leveled against

---

[54]   Isabel of Bavaria (1371–1435) was the queen consort of Charles VI of France, regent during his periodic bouts of insanity; she was Louis XI's grandmother, Anne of France's great-grandmother. See especially Rachel Gibbons, "Isabeau of Bavaria, Queen of France (1385–1422): The Creation of an Historical Villainess," *Transactions of the Royal Historical Society*, 6th ser., 6 (1996), 51–73.

Margaret of Anjou was Anne's cousin (see "Introduction," 4). For the connection between her political role and allegations of adultery and promiscuity, see Helen E. Maurer, *Margaret of Anjou: Queenship and Power in Late Medieval England* (Woodbridge: The Boydell Press, 2003), *passim*, especially 175–6. She would have provided Anne of France a personal, visible, and potent model of the dangers of sexual innuendo. In 1470, Margaret's son Prince Edward was married to Anne Neville at Amboise; after the battle of Tewkesbury, Margaret was held prisoner in the Tower, from which she was ransomed by Louis XI. Margaret of Anjou lived as his pensioner in France until her death in August 1482, just one year before Anne of France began her "rule" of France. About Margaret's struggle and eventual failure, Maurer concludes that "as a woman of her world, she could not dispense with ingrained notions of queenship or of what constituted her gendered

Anne of France. A great deal of resentment over the extent of her power and control focused on her sex, but the usual tactic of attacking her sexuality was never employed. No breath of scandal suggested she was guilty of any sexual impropriety, or that Suzanne, born after so many years of childless marriage, was illegitimate. In controlling her personal conduct, then, a princess could remove a potent weapon from the hands of those who would discredit her. Since she must live in the world, Suzanne will "encounter the bad as well as the good," including men whose aim is to dishonor her. But she must not draw back from the world, no matter how many dangers threaten. Anne recommends control and vigilance rather than isolation because "the thing most highly commended is that which has been in the fire yet cannot be scorched (or worse) . . . or that which has been in the mire of this world yet cannot be soiled in any way." Suzanne will be assailed but must be unassailable: "Always bear yourself honorably, with a cool and assured manner, a humble gaze, and a quiet word; be constant and firm every day, to each proposal, without bending."

Anne's advice thus reflects both her own experience and her unblinking look at human nature, advice that is either cynical or frank, depending on your point-of-view. "For of men one can, in general, say this: They are ungrateful, fickle, deceptive and deceiving, avoiders of danger, eager to gain," Machiavelli would later write.[55] Anne's advice comes out of an equally blunt assessment of her experiences in dealing with others. Never confide in people, she tells Suzanne, because they will not keep her secrets; "The world today is corrupt in this regard, so you do not know whom to trust." Relationships are rarely disinterested; "among a thousand, rarely is there even one who will serve another solely out of love," without some "more practical consideration," like money or advancement. And even if Suzanne were to try to "follow the right path," others would do nothing but "mock" her attempts "in various ways, so corrupt is the world and, in this case, so disordered." There is no point in trying to change people, for they will remain "incorrigible," and so "you waste your time thinking to chastise them; there is no remedy unless you give them leave and dispatch them immediately." And so, Anne concludes, "Never trust such people, and if you find them around you, send them away"—but do it "graciously."

As a "feminine and weak creature," then, Suzanne's life will be a difficult one, as her mother well knows. Thus it is important to avoid

___

place. It is her adherence to these standards, rather than a mythic disregard for them, that is striking" (208).

[55] *The Prince*, 52.

unnecessary complications. It is "the greatest misfortune in the world," she writes, when a wise person "is subjected to the government of a fool." Therefore, she cautions, "protect yourself, as you can, from being so subjected." But if Suzanne finds herself in such a situation, as she almost inevitably will, she must avoid any blame or censure for the mistakes of those around her; she needs to correct their behavior, but at the same time she must avoid offending them. Thus she should not blame them, reprimand them, or confront them, but act "subtly," "sweetly"—and indirectly—by distracting them or manipulating them, "by proposing something new, for example, or by making a pleasant suggestion or by praising the suggestions of others or by showing your approval of some other action or deed."

As far as her daughter's conduct in court, Anne cautions Suzanne about observing the proprieties: "it is not right for a young woman to meddle in or busy herself with too many things." She must conduct herself carefully: "And so that all goes smoothly, I counsel you to mind your own business, without asking about anything or wanting to know anything about the affairs or conduct of others." But when it happens that Suzanne "know[s] something," she must be discreet; "take care that you do not reveal it," Anne warns. If someone asks about the extent of her knowledge, "do not admit to knowing anything." Such silence, Anne claims, is well justified by authority: "As Socrates says, a man or woman of great rank should never reveal the secret of another as long as there is no harm in concealing it and especially as long as it does no harm to your master or mistress." "Everybody recognizes how praiseworthy it is" for a prince to "live a life of integrity" and "to keep his word" without "relying on craftiness," Machiavelli writes, but a successful prince must know "how to employ cunning to confuse and disorient other men."[56] Anne suggests her own brand of "disorientation": "It is important to control your bearing, your expressions, your words, your sentiments, your thoughts, your desires, your wishes, and your passions," she cautions. Regardless of whether life brings fortune or misfortune, "never openly reveal yourself by any outward sign, semblance, or circumstance, or by your relationships, or by any other means."

Concealment is thus necessary for the politic life, but it is not enough. One of the most famous questions debated in *The Prince* is "whether it is better to be loved than feared, or the reverse."[57] Machiavelli, of course, concludes that, "as far as being feared and

---

[56]   *The Prince*, 53.
[57]   *The Prince*, 51.

loved is concerned, since men decide for themselves whom they
love, and rulers decide whom they fear, a wise ruler should rely on
the emotion he can control, and not on the one he cannot."[58] The
question is not as easy for a princess as it is for the prince. Given her
"weak female nature," she cannot so readily "rely on the emotion"
she can control, but Anne does suggest that a woman can manipulate
her love to gain some measure of control. Her daughter should
"make sure" that she is always "pleasant to all and loved by all." To
this end she must always take care "to please all others according to
their rank," she must "take care to please everyone" so that "no one
will have reason to hate" her, she should "take care to speak kindly,
to respond graciously, to converse about honest and pleasant subjects, and to be agreeable to all, according to their rank," she should
"always be humble and gracious" so that she is "always loved more
and better by everyone." And like Machiavelli, who instructs his
would-be prince that "he must take care to avoid being hated," Anne
also insists that Suzanne act so "that no one ever has any reason to
hate" her. It is very easy to dismiss Anne's insistence on the need to
be loved and never hated as conventionally gendered behavior, but it
can also be politically effective. In her own years of power, *Madame*
was resented but never hated, and she certainly took care to please
her enemies as well as she could, appealing to their self-interest
whenever possible to gain their support.

Much of her advice to Suzanne, in fact, shows how a woman can
avoid being hated. Among the most conventional of her instructions
concern a woman's clothing. Some of it is practical advice—avoid
outrageous fashions—some of it motherly excess—dress warmly or
you will catch cold and die—but most of it is linked to Anne's
concern that Suzanne avoid provoking envy. Her advice itself, then,
is *conventional*, standard conduct-book fare about avoiding extravagance in dress, but this advice reflects *unconventional* concerns
because it springs not from warnings about female vanity and pride,
but from her experience that such extravagance produces envy.[59] As
she warns Suzanne, "Many weak-willed fools are envious of everyone,

---

[58] *The Prince*, 53.

[59] In *The Treasure of the City of Ladies*, for example, Christine de Pizan
warns women against extravagance in dress, primarily because it reflects the
"great pride that infects many women," but also because "it is a sin and it
displeases God to be so attentive to one's own body." It's also a waste of money
and sets a bad example for other women; only "fifth" on the list of reasons for
women of rank to avoid extravagance is because it provokes envy (59–62 and
149–53).

but especially of women who are accomplished and of great rank." Such envy harms all women, even those "who are good and without flaws"; some people "are so poisoned by envy that when they see good in other women, even one of their own relatives, they hate them so much that they revile them everywhere they go." Such envy will produce hatred that can have disastrous consequences:

It is the condition and nature of the envious that, if they cannot satisfactorily revenge themselves on those they envy, then they want them dead or have them killed—and thus they are revenged. But they arrange this so no one is aware of it, because such people only act covertly and foully, and in their malice use subtle means so that they do not discover themselves to honest people and so that the honest do not see their machinations. The envious contrive great falsehoods about the goodness and honor of those whom they envy, and simple people believe their lies and spread them, certifying them to be true; thus it comes to pass that the honor of many is damaged for no reason, all because of envy. Therefore, my daughter, make sure you are not thus surprised. . . .

Like Machiavelli, who states that the prince's "choice as to whom to employ as his advisers is of foremost importance," Anne instructs Suzanne to find and keep good counselors.[60] For Machiavelli, "The easiest way of assessing a ruler's ability is to look at those who are members of his inner circle. If they are competent and reliable, then you can be sure he is wise, for he has known both how to recognize their ability and to keep them faithful." Suzanne, by contrast, may not always be able to choose her own advisers. When she is married, she must care to "earn the love" of her husband's lords and friends, not only because she owes her husband "nothing less than compliance and obedience," but also so that she does not "provoke his folly" and so that she will not be blamed for his mistakes or "bad government." To this end, she must "act demurely" when she is in the company of her husband's friends and supporters and make them her own by "doing what you think will be agreeable to them and taking their advice in your affairs without doing anything on your own" because arrogance will produce resentment. "Stay close to your friends," Anne advises, "taking their advice and, as you can, helping them with their interests and necessities." To maintain their friendship, she might even have to "help them conceal their faults," but that

---

[60] *The Prince*, 70–73. Machiavelli devotes two chapters, 22 and 23, to "those whom rulers employ as advisers" and to avoiding "sycophants."

is necessary because, as she notes: "as the proverb goes, in prosperity you will find friends enough, but in adversity, few."

Only the arrogant ignore good advice, Anne observes, again noting a bit of common wisdom: "you are not a fool unless you think you are wise." But just as Machiavelli acknowledges that the only way for a prince to get the best out of an adviser is to "consider" the adviser's interests, "heaping honors on him, enriching him, placing him in his debt, ensuring he receives public recognition, so that he sees that he cannot do better without him," Anne advises her daughter that she should not only heed her friends and counselors' good advice but she should reward them, "helping them with their interests and necessities."[61] But caution is always needed. One of Machiavelli's most shocking assertions is that while "there are always reasons why you might want to seize people's property," a prince should "keep [his] hands off other people's property; for men are quicker to forget the death of their father than the loss of their inheritance."[62] Anne is more restrained. Suzanne should not "acquire anything unjustly," nor should she "rejoice in what has been wrongly gained."

And Suzanne must also be prepared for what the future might bring her, for in the last sections of her *enseignements* Anne addresses the likelihood that her daughter might herself be called upon to govern the vast Bourbon inheritance her mother had carved out for her.[63] Anne begins with an acknowledgement of the political realities of the aristocratic life: a woman will find herself called upon to take charge if her husband dies, if her husband goes to war, or if he is otherwise called away "into danger." In such situations, "like many other young women," Suzanne must be prepared to take up the reigns of power. Her mother's advice is succinct: "govern wisely." She must avoid the extremes of prostration on the one hand or rising too eagerly and easily to the occasion on the other. But about women's roles, in such situations, there is no doubt: "When it comes to the government of their lands and affairs, they must depend only on themselves; when it comes to sovereignty, they must not cede power to anyone." A woman must be prepared to protect herself "from deceitful and presumptuous" members of her own household, as well as from the gossip and slander that might be occasioned by working too closely with them. While thus taking control absolutely, she must nevertheless seek out and accept the wise counsel that

[61] *The Prince*, 71.
[62] *The Prince*, 52.
[63] Sections XXVII [29]–XXX [32].

Anne has recommended so strongly. Given Anne's consideration of the subject for government in the final sections of her *Lessons*, the reason for her return to the topic of chastity at this point is clear. What seems confused at first—a return to a subject she had earlier dealt with—now makes sense, for, as we have seen, the link between a woman's sex and her sexuality is critical. When she is alone and in a position of power, her "honor" must be preserved "in all purity and cleanness." Any impropriety, or rumor of impropriety, is doubly dangerous, and thus Anne's return to the subject, accompanied this time by specific advice about how to deal with men who can compromise her reputation.

In pointing out the similarities here between Anne of France's princess and Machiavelli's prince, I am not suggesting that the comparison is either simple or straightforward. Just as there are many difficulties in interpreting *The Prince*, the instructions Anne offers in her *Lessons* are confused, open to multiple interpretations, and often contradictory. The princess must live within conventions but not conventionally. Thus she must take care she does not provoke envy by her attire, while at the same time she must use her clothing to differentiate herself from other members of her household and to signal her status—no other woman's dress should approach hers in its costliness and elegance. The princess must not talk too much, but neither should she be too silent, and she must use her conversation to mark out her favor but also to mask her disfavor. She should never lie, but neither should she reveal what she knows, even if she is asked, and she should conceal the faults and weaknesses of others. She must be controlled, to the point of never moving a muscle unnecessarily, yet she must use every gesture to indicate not only her self-control but her dominance of everyone else on every occasion. She must be absolutely obedient to her husband, even while always on guard to protect herself from his folly and to ensure she is not blamed for his mistakes, prepared always to act even while she seems never willing to act. And while she must not trust in any "chastity, strength, or perfection" she thinks she may have, she is as capable of self-control as any man and has, in herself, the ability and the good judgment to act virtuously. What I take to be the most clear and concise statement of her method is, in fact, a perfect example of the delicate balance that is attempted in her *enseignements* for Suzanne: "Wise men say that you should have eyes to notice everything yet to see nothing, ears to hear everything yet to know nothing, and a tongue to answer everyone yet to say nothing prejudicial to anyone."

In assigning this insight to "wise men," Anne demonstrates the paradoxical nature of her efforts to educate Suzanne as she alternates between attributing her advice to wise, often nameless, men—"according to one philosopher," "a certain philosopher says"—and claiming it for herself—"I counsel you," "I advise you." But rather than *over*looking these contradictions to find her "meaning," I think that we must look *to* them, for we find her meaning in these "faults" and in the fissures and chasms that result from them. As Evelyne Berriot Salvador argues, in such contradictions we can find the "birth" of women's ways of writing.[64] Because the very act of writing is "a transgression of women's 'natural role,' which is not to speak to one another but to silence themselves, not to reveal themselves but to conceal themselves," a woman who chooses to write must "appear to assume" the "rules of the game," even as she breaks them.[65] The "artifices" that she employs "establish the deliberate use of disguise as the first principle of writing," her act of writing thus becoming a *rewriting* of what it means to be a woman.[66] And so, I would argue, as Anne of France struggles to teach her daughter what it means to be a woman, we need to look with particular attention at the contradictions and confusions that are part of that struggle. We must listen to what is said, but we must also hear what is unsaid.

The world of the *Lessons* is curiously but significantly free of male control. For all the attention paid to Suzanne's life as a daughter, paternal authority is absent. While a wife must be obedient, the husband she must obey is an elusive presence, prone to folly, mistakes, and, of course, absence, either because of war or death. As a mother, Suzanne must pay particular attention to the rearing of daughters; sons are never mentioned. In this context, one of Anne's *enseignements* is particularly noteworthy. It is a reminder for her daughter not to forget the "glory and honor" of her "lineage"; she admonishes her daughter not only to serve her family but to "value highly your own ancestors, those from whom *you* are descended," in particular honoring the women who had preceded her. A noble woman remembers the lines of blood and intimacy that bind women together and in remembering the women to whom she is related, she does them honor. Only foolish women think nothing of their foremothers—of their mothers and grandmothers, of their aunts and sisters. In

---

[64] ' "Les Femmes et les pratiques de l'écriture de Christine de Pisan à Marie de Gournay", 59'.
[65] Berriot Salvador, 60.
[66] Berriot Salvador, 59.

Virginia Woolf's words, Suzanne should "think back through her mother."[67]

While Anne may have outlived those of her own generation, and even her own daughter, she shaped the lives of many influential women. At the moment of her death, two of them had taken their own places on the stage of early modern power and politics: Margaret of Austria, whom Anne had raised and educated for ten years, was regent of the Netherlands for her nephew, the Habsburg emperor Charles V, while Louise of Savoy, who had been sent by her father to Anne of France when the girl was seven, had already served as regent of France for her son, Francis I, and would be called upon a second time to fulfill that role.[68] They were only two of the generation of women she had influenced; in Brantôme's words, "there were no ladies or daughters of great houses in her time who did not receive lessons from her."[69] Having shaped the next generation and having distilled her principles into her *Lessons*, Anne of France had become a "mother" for women to "think back through." I would like to think that in this she found a measure of satisfaction.

---

[67] See "Preface," vii.
[68] Jansen, 81–96, 181–93. The 1535 edition of Anne's *Lessons* was dedicated to Louise's daughter, Marguerite of Angoulême, whose own daughter would rule Navarre in her own right.
[69] Wormley, 218.

Appendix I

Louis XI, Anne of France, and the Regency Question

Two questions are commonly raised about Louis XI's arrangements for his son at the time of his death. First, why did he decide against a formal regency? Second, why did he put his son in his daughter's guardianship instead of his wife's?

In response to the first question, the answer provided by historian John Bridge is most sensible.[1] At the time of Louis XI's death on 30 August 1483, the *dauphin* Charles was just over thirteen years old, somewhat sickly, and completely inexperienced. By the terms of a statute of 1374, the age and legal majority of a king of France was defined as the heir's attainment of his "fourteenth year." There was some ambiguity in this law. As Bridge notes, "If [the wording of the statute] meant that a King attained his legal majority when he entered upon his fourteenth year, then Charles was legally of age, and no Regency would be required." But "it was possible so to construe the ordinance as to postpone a sovereign's majority until he reached his fourteenth birthday, and from this occasion Charles was still removed by the space of nearly a year." There was "no binding precedent" for the king to cite, and the ambiguity of the situation would almost surely result in disagreement and dissent after his death. By avoiding a regency, the king avoided any arguments over interpretation and, more important, any early termination of his daughter's guardianship, which extended into 1491, well after Charles VIII's "fourteenth year," whichever way that ambiguous phrase were to be interpreted.

The designation of a regent was also made difficult by the choice of a regent. Bridge indicated that a regency would "belong to the first Prince of the Blood," in this case Louis of Orléans, who was also the heir presumptive and, thus, not necessarily the most disinterested of candidates. But an obvious candidate for regent was Charlotte of Savoy, the queen consort and mother of the *dauphin*; recent scholarship has, in fact, focused on the regency as what one historian has

---

[1] For what follows, see John S. C. Bridge, *A History of France from the Death of Louis XI*, vol. 1: *Reign of Charles VIII, Regency of Anne of Beaujeu, 1483–1493* (1921; rpt. New York, Octagon Books, 1978), 26–27.

called a "vocation" for royal women.[2] While the so-called Salic law denied women (like Anne of France herself) the right to inherit the crown of France, it did not deny them access to power. It seemed, instead, to assure them a place in government, for as the law of succession developed in France, a corresponding body of law on the regency was also formulated. Women might be barred from sovereignty, but their potential and the ability to act as regent was recognized: their very "nature" as women assured that could be relied on to defend the throne for their husbands or sons, and thus they were preferred to men in the role of regent for a young, absent, or incapacitated king.[3]

By the late fifteenth century, there had been several female regents in France. As André Poulet notes, queens had shared in government from the time of Hugh Capet, but the first woman to serve officially as regent was Adele of Champagne, third wife of Louis VII. Her fifteen-year-old son Philip II resisted her role when he succeeded to the throne in 1180, but when he prepared to go on crusade ten years later, he entrusted his mother and her brother, the archbishop of Rheims, to act as regent of his son, the future Louis VIII.[4] When Louis VIII succeeded to the throne, he named his wife Blanche of Castile as regent for his son, Louis IX. Poulet discusses Blanche's "absolute power" as regent: she "legislated, dealt with foreign powers, waged war, arranged marriages." "In short," he concludes, she "imposed herself as sovereign of the realm."[5] The king "recalled" his mother "to affairs of state" when he went on crusade in 1248. Blanche's great-grandson Philip IV also arranged for a female regent; he named his wife Jeanne of Navarre as regent in the eventuality he died before their son Louis X

---

2   See André Poulet, "Capetian Women and the Regency: The Genesis of a Vocation," in John Carmi Parsons, ed., *Medieval Queenship* (New York: St. Martin's Press, 1993), 93–116.

3   On the development of Salic law, see John Milton Potter, "The Development and Significance of the Salic Law of the French," *English Historical Review* 52 (1937), 235–53 and Ralph E. Giesey, "The Juristic Basis of the Dynastic Right to the French Throne," *Transactions of the American Philosophical Society*, n.s. 51 (1961), 3–47.

   On the developing law of the regency and the preference for a woman to act as regent, a good place to start is Fanny Cosandey, "De lance en quenouille. La place de la reigne dans l'État moderne (14ᵉ–17ᵉ siècles)," *Annales* 52 (1997), 799–820.

4   Poulet, 108. See also Marion F. Facinger, "A Study of Medieval Queenship: Capetian France, 987–1237," *Studies in Medieval and Renaissance History* 5 (1968), 8–9.

5   Poulet, 110.

was old enough to succeed him.[6] In 1338, Philip VI named his wife Jeanne of Burgundy to function as regent when he went to war, while his grandson, Charles V, perhaps fearing the power of his wife Jeanne of Bourbon, split the regency between his wife, named as guardian of their son, and his two brothers.[7] In 1395, Charles VI named his wife Isabel of Bavaria as guardian of their son, the future Charles VII (Louis XI's father). As Charles began to suffer periodic bouts of insanity, her role was expanded in a series of ordinances; by 1403 she was "acknowledged as the leader of a new regency council," empowered to mediate and to deal with matters of finance in addition to acting as principal guardian of the *dauphin*.

As queen and regent, Isabel of Bavaria was vilified and condemned for her political ambitions. As Rachel Gibbons notes, she was accused of "adultery, incest, moral corruption, treason, avarice and profligacy," her "reputed beauty" used as " 'proof' of her evil," her sexual activity necessarily resulting in her "neglect" of her children.[8] A similar tactic had been used to discredit Louis XI's cousin, Margaret of Anjou, the wife of Henry VI of England; during the king's incapacity and capture, she attempted to claim the regency in order to act on behalf of their son, Prince Edward; in order to prevent her regency and to discredit the queen, Yorkist propaganda focused on her sexual promiscuity and denied the prince was the king's son, claiming instead he was a bastard, the product of one of Margaret's illicit sexual encounters.[9] What seems to have made both of these female regents particularly vulnerable to attack was their foreignness.[10] Louis XI was faced with a similar example in the person of his sister-in-law, Bona of Savoy, the queen of France's younger sister.[11] In 1476, when her husband was assassinated, she

---

[6] Poulet, 112.

[7] Poulet, 112–14.

[8] "Isabeau of Bavaria, Queen of France (1385–1422): The Creation of an Historical Villainess," *Transactions of the Royal Historical Society*, 6th ser., 6 (1996), 54.

[9] For the connection between Margaret of Anjou's political role and allegations of adultery and promiscuity, see Helen E. Maurer, *Margaret of Anjou: Queenship and Power in Late Medieval England* (Woodbridge: The Boydell Press, 2003), *passim*, but especially 175–76.

[10] Although she is writing about another queen of France, Catherine de' Medici, Nicola M. Sutherland is particularly useful here; see "Catherine de Medici: The Legend of the Wicked Italian Queen," in her *Princes, Politics and Religion, 1547–1589* (London: Hambledon Press, 1984), 237–48.

[11] When Galeazzo Maria Sforza succeeded his father as duke of Milan in 1466, he was at Louis XI's court in France, where he was negotiating a marriage with

became regent of Milan for her son Giangaleazzo, but by 1480 she had been removed from the regency by Ludovico, her husband's brother, who acted first as regent, but then took the title of duke of Milan for himself. Bona had traveled to the French court, seeking the king's support for an attempt to retake the regency, but Louis XI had failed to offer it.

Thus the choice of regent was a problematic one for the king. In deciding against naming a regent for his son, Louis XI still faced the prospect of naming a guardian, one who could function *as* regent without having the title *of* regent. Why he rejected Louis of Orléans, the heir presumptive, is clear enough, and given the duke's rebellion during the first years of Charles VIII's nominal reign, this rejection seems to have been well justified. Why he rejected Charlotte of Savoy, often debated, is also clear, however we judge her abilities, since the example of her sister had just offered the king yet another instance of the problems involved in female regency. Had he named Charlotte of Savoy "guardian" for the *dauphin*, she would have been vulnerable on two fronts, her sex and her foreignness. She might have withstood attacks against her personal morality, but she could never have denied her foreignness, and with a force as volatile as Louis of Orléans, the king did not need to hand him a weapon to use against the "guardian" of his son.

While the choice of his daughter as "guardian" may be, as some have called it, "unprecedented," it seems to have been the most obvious in the circumstances. Regardless of her abilities, she did not have the disabilities of the king's other choices. As a woman, his daughter could not inherit the throne of France, and thus she posed no threat to Charles. As a married woman, she was not as exposed as her widowed mother to the attacks of a woman without male "protection." As a Frenchwoman, she was not under suspicion as a foreigner.

Bona, the king's sister-in-law. When Galeazzo traveled back to Milan as the new duke, he was accompanied by his new wife, Bona of Savoy (c. 1450?–1505).

There were many alliances between Louis XI and his wife's family. Charlotte of Savoy's brother Amadeus IX of Savoy was married to the king's sister Yolande, as we have seen ("Introduction," 4). The queen's sister Marguerite (b. c. 1446) was married to Pierre de Luxembourg, connétable de Saint-Pol; Agnes (b. 1457) was married to François de Dunois, comte de Longueville; her brother Philip's first marriage was to Marguerite of Bourbon (their daughter was Louise of Savoy).

Appendix II

Unpublished Letters from Anne of France

Pauline Matarasso incorporates many of Anne of France's surviving letters into her *Queen's Mate*, including three from Suzanne of Bourbon to her parents, one to her father and two to her mother.[1] Matarasso uses these three very short letters as evidence that it "is obvious that Suzanne was the apple of her father's eye and loved him passionately in return, that he was her playmate, companion and confidant" and that, by contrast, her "relations with her mother were much more formal and reserved," so much more formal and reserved that Suzanne "obviously had difficulty in finding something to say." While reaching these judgments, Matarasso does recognize that there is a danger in "inferring too much from the patchy evidence the past has left us."[2]

But as we have seen, Matarasso finds the *Lessons* "singularly lacking in love, almost shockingly so." The only evidence offered to support her assertion is that Louis IX, when composing his instructions for his daughter, addressed her as *chiere fille*, "dear daughter," while Anne addresses Suzanne with "only the cool 'ma fille' [my daughter] throughout."[3] Leaving aside the question of whether "dear daughter" expresses more love than "my daughter," leaving aside the more important question of whether any *professions of love* are necessarily *proof of love*, and, perhaps most important, leaving aside the question of why we should demand or expect love in a text authored by a woman, I include here extracts

[1] See Pauline Matarasso, *The Queen's Mate: Three Women of Power in France on the Eve of the Renaissance* (Burlington, VT: Ashgate Publishing, 2001), 195.

[2] Matarasso, 196.

[3] Matarasso, 194. The formulaic *chier fils* is also used to introduce each one of the thirty-three instructions he addressed to his son Philip; see David O'Connell, *The Teachings of Saint Louis: A Critical Text* (Chapel Hill, NC: The University of North Carolina Press, 1972), 55–60. It is worth mentioning here that in the sixteenth-century printed edition of her *enseignements*, Anne does address Suzanne as "my very dear daughter" on one occasion (Section XIX), this singular instance attracting much more of the reader's attention than the regular use of the phrase in Louis IX's lists of instructions does.

of letters from Anne of France that do not appear in Matarasso's book.

The letters are in Anne's own hand, addressed to Madame du Bouchage, Suzanne's governess, and they seem to have been written while Suzanne is still a baby, probably in the first several months after her birth. Like the manuscript of Anne of France's *Lessons*, these letters were found in the Imperial Library of St. Petersburg; they are extracted in the notes of the multi-volume history of the Bourbon dukes.[4] I have not traveled to Russia to transcribe these letters myself; I offer them here as additional insight into Anne of France and in the hope that some future scholar will trace the originals.

The first letter is addressed to *ma commère*; there is no simple English translation of this title, which means, literally, "my co-mother." Anne writes, "I have received the letters you have written me and see by them that my daughter is doing very well, which makes me very happy. I pray you continue always to keep me informed, and you will make me happy. . . ." There is an ellipsis at this point, indicating that the something has been omitted. The extract continues: "It gives me great pleasure to have news often."

A second letter again begins with the salutation *ma commère*: "I see by your letters that my daughter grows day by day, which makes me very happy. I pray you, as often as you can, send me news and letters."[5]

A third letter seems to be presented nearly in its entirety—there is one ellipse—and is written in response to the "news" that the baby had a little fever. It too begins *ma commère*:

> I am very relieved at the news you have sent about my daughter, and that, as you wrote, the brief illness she had was the result of teething. If her nurse [evidently Suzanne's wetnurse] were a little sick, I do not believe that you would hide it from me any more than you would hide my daughter's illness. I do not want to hear that you have done otherwise. I am worried by the letter that Master Albert has written me, however; he found my daughter a little warm, and indicated that, if it were left up to him, he would say that

---

4   All the letters included here are found in Jean-Marie de la Mure, *Histoire des ducs de Bourbon et des comtes de Forez* . . . , ed. R. Chantelauze (Paris: A. Montbrison, 1868), 2:429–30 nn. According to Chantelauze, the "autograph letters" are from Ms. Fr. N. 2930.

5   Here Anne indicates that news can be transmitted by messengers as well as by letters.

the cause was the nurse, which I find very strange coming from a doctor if he had not found the nurse suffering or fevered. Therefore, my dear [Anne repeats *ma commère* here], I pray that you will immediately summon Catherine and check her milk for yourself to see whether she has a fever or whether there has been a change [in her milk]; find out whether the nights are going well, whether she is warm, or whether she is otherwise uncomfortable, and if you find nothing . . . do not at all change her meat; I am sending Master Milon to you—he is leaving Saturday—and he will tell you what to do.[6] And I pray that you will write immediately, telling me at length about my daughter and her nurse.

One further letter is included here, this one from Anne to her father, written in 1482 or 1483. Matarasso prints most of this letter, but omits the last sentence and the closer which show this is a more "formal" letter than Matarasso suggests.

My lord,

I see from the letter you have written me and from the letters of your doctors that you have gout—the greatest sorrow I have when I know you are ill is that I am not with you. I pray, my lord, that you make sure [the messengers] you send me keep me informed about your health for, by my faith, I am not at all easy on the day when I have [no news].[7] Your children are in very good cheer, praying God to give you health and long life.

From the hand of your very humble and very obedient daughter,

Anne[8]

---

[6] The ellipsis here is in the printed edition; it is impossible to tell whether something has been omitted or whether the ellipsis is Anne's.

   Anne tells Madam du Bouchage not to change the nurse's *viandes*, literally her meat, but it is possible we should understand that there should be no change in the nurse's diet until Master Milon arrives to check things out.

[7] *the messengers* Anne actually writes "those who come"; *no news* Anne actually writes "when I have none."

[8] Matarasso, 11.

Select Bibliography

Relatively little has been written about Anne of France and her lessons, and much of what has been written is in French. This bibliography lists both English and French sources, with those in French so identified for the reader.

Biographies of Anne of France

Chabannes, Hedwige de and Isabelle de Linarès. *Anne de Beaujeu: "Ce fut ung roy."* Paris: Crépin Leblond, 1955. Thorough and readable account of Anne of France's life, relying to a great extent on D'Orliac's biography (see below); contains a chapter assessing Anne's political influence, especially on Louise of Savoy and Margaret of Austria, and another on Anne's *Lessons*. No documentation. (In French.)

D'Orliac, Jehanne. *Anne de Beaujeu, roi de France.* Paris: Librarie Plon, 1926. Useful and readable, though somewhat dated, account of Anne of France's life, particularly valuable for the chapter on her early life. No documentation. (In French.)

Lauwe, Marc Chombart de. *Anne de Beaujeu: ou la passion du pouvoir.* Paris: Librairie Jules Tallandier, 1980. A relatively scholarly biography, particularly useful for its use of primary-source material; detailed family trees. (In French.)

Pradel, Pierre. *Anne de France, 1461–1522.* Paris: Editions Publisud, 1986. Completed in 1974, shortly before Pradel's death, though not published until 1986; a thorough and scholarly account of Anne of France's life and the politics of France during the period, including detailed family trees. (In French.)

Salmon, J. H. M. "The Regent and the Duchess: Anne de Beaujeu and Anne de Bretagne." *History Today* 16 (1960), 341–48. A brief but readable account of the "rivalry" between the "strongly ambitious and fiercely self-willed" Anne of France and her sister-in-law Anne of Brittany, twice queen of France.

Multiple biographies that include Anne of France

Jansen, Sharon L. *The Monstrous Regiment of Women: Female Rulers in Early Modern Europe.* New York: Palgrave Macmillan, 2002. Multiple biography of fifteenth- and sixteenth-century women rulers, including an extended discussion of Anne of France as well as her influence on ruling women in succeeding generations.

Matarasso, Pauline. *The Queen's Mate: Three Women of Power in France on the Eve of the Renaissance*. Burlington, VT: Ashgate Publishing, 2001. A well-documented multiple biography, focusing on Anne of France, Anne of Brittany, and Louise of Savoy; includes excellent comments on Anne's *Lessons* (*passim*).

Montaigu, Henry. *La Guerre des dames: La Fin des féodaux*. Paris: Olivier Orban, 1981. A multiple biography focusing on Anne of France, Anne of Brittany, and Louise of Savoy but including significant discussion as well of Jeanne of France, Margaret of Austria, and Claude of France, among others, in its history of the "war of women" at the end of the Middle Ages; many detailed family trees. No documentation. (In French.)

Critical analyses of Anne of France's political role

Bridge, John S. C. *Reign of Charles VIII, Regency of Anne of Beaujeu, 1483–1493*. Vol. 1 of *A History of France from the Death of Louis XI*. 1921. Reprint, New York: Octagon Books, 1978. Most comprehensive analysis of Anne of France's government in English, relying extensively on primary-source material and the ground-breaking work of Pélicier (see below).

Pélicier, Paul. *Essai sur le gouvernement de la Dame de Beaujeu, 1483–1491*. Chartres: Imprimerie Édouard Garnier, 1882. Scholarly and influential study of Anne's political role during the years she acted as "guardian" for Charles VIII, concluding that Anne did, in fact, rule France during this period; despite its date, Pélicier's study remains an essential work. (In French.)

Editions of *Lessons for My Daughter*

Chazaud, A[lphonse]-M[artial]. *Les Enseignements d'Anne de France, Duchesse de Bourbonnois et d'Auvergne à sa fille Susanne de Bourbon. . . .* Moulins: C. Desrosiers, 1878. Reprint, Marseille: Laffitte Reprints, 1978. The only surviving evidence of the manuscript version of Anne of France's *Lessons*, Chazaud's edition has been the sole reliable source for all readers of Anne's text.

Viple, Joseph. *Les Enseignements d'Anne de France*. Moulins: Crepin-Leblond, 1935. A peculiar "book" that presents a version of Anne of France's *Lessons*, translating some passages into modern French, quoting (often incorrectly) large chunks of Chazaud's edition of Anne's text, and rearranging the whole. No documentation. (In French.)

Critical studies of *Lessons for My Daughter*

Bornstein, Diane. *The Lady in the Tower: Medieval Courtesy Literature for Women*. Hamden: Archon Books, 1983. General overview of conduct literature for women; limits its discussion of Anne of France's text to her discussion of Suzanne's role as wife and mother (71–74).

Hentsch, Alice A. *De la littérature didactique du moyen âge s'adressant spécialement aux femmes*. Cahors, France: A. Coueslant, 1903. Remarkable analysis of a wide range of didactic literature for women, including a detailed summary of Anne of France's text (199–207), organized by topic: religious and moral precepts, love and marriage, widowhood; the education of children; clothing; serving as a *demoiselle d'honneur*; managing a household and servants. (In French.)

Jordan, Constance. *Renaissance Feminism: Literary Texts and Political Models*. Ithaca, NY: Cornell University Press, 1990. While her discussion of Anne of France's *Lessons* is relatively brief (95–100), Jordan is the only scholar to have considered the political implications of Anne's advice to Suzanne.

Krueger, Roberta L. "*Chascune selon son estat*: Women's Education and Social Class in the Conduct Books of Christine de Pizan and Anne de France." *Papers on French Seventeenth Century Literature* 24.46 (1997), 19–34. Assumes that Anne of France's text is directly influenced by and modeled on Christine de Pizan's *Livre de trois vertus* (*The Treasure of the City of Ladies*); concludes that Anne envisioned a "limited aristocratic audience" for her work, while Christine's "may have empowered some readers to overstep boundaries that were in flux and to manipulate their social improvement."

Willard, Charity Cannon. "Anne de France, Reader of Christine de Pizan." In Glenda K. McLeod, ed., *The Reception of Christine de Pizan from the Fifteenth through the Nineteenth Centuries: Visitors to the City*, 59–70. Lewiston, NY: Edwin Mellen Press, 1991. Seminal study of Anne of France's text; while specific references to the *enseignements* are very few, Willard's study is a principal influence on all the critical studies that have followed, particularly for her identification of Anne's *Lessons* as an example of conduct literature and for her claim that Anne's text is modeled on Christine de Pizan's *The Treasure of the City of Ladies*.

Winn, Colette H. "'*De mères en filles*': Les manuels d'éducation sous l'Ancien Régime." *Atlantis* 19.1 (1983), 23–29. Examines three centuries of portraits of "ideal woman/mother," focusing on Christine de Pizan's *The Treasure of the City of Ladies*, Anne's *Lessons*, and Jeanne de Schomberg's *Reglement donné par une Dame de haute qualité à Mxxx, sa petite-fille* (published in 1698). (In French.)

——. "La *Dignitas Mulieris*: Les Enjeux idéologiques d'une appropriation du xve au xviie siècle." *Études Littéraires* 27.2 (1994), 11–24. Examines the "long tradition of didactic works for women" that paint a portrait of the "ideal woman"; in addition to the three texts noted above (Winn, 1983), adds a brief discussion of Gabrielle de Coignard's *Œuvres chrestiennes* (1594). (In French.)

Index

Library of Medieval Women

Already published

Christine de Pizan's Letter of Othea to Hector, *Jane Chance*, 1990

Writings of Margaret of Oingt, Medieval Prioress and Mystic, *Renate Blumenfeld-Kosinski*, 1990

Saint Bride and her Book: Birgitta of Sweden's *Revelations*, *Julia Bolton Holloway*, 1992; new edition 2000

The Memoirs of Helene Kottanner (1439–1440), *Maya Bijvoet Williamson*, 1998

The Writings of Teresa de Cartagena, *Dayle Seidenspinner-Núñez*, 1998

Julian of Norwich, Revelations of Divine Love and The Motherhood of God, *Frances Beer*, 1998

Hrotsvit of Gandersheim: A Florilegium of her Works, *Katharina M. Wilson*, 1998

Hildegard of Bingen: On Natural Philosophy and Medicine: Selections from *Cause et Cure, Margret Berger*, 1999

Women Saints' Lives in Old English Prose, *Leslie A. Donovan*, 1999

Angela of Foligno's Memorial, *Cristina Mazzoni*, 2000

The Letters of the Rožmberk Sisters, *John M. Klassen*, 2001

The Life of Saint Douceline, a Beguine of Provence, *Kathleen Garay and Madeleine Jeay*, 2001

Agnes Blannbekin, Viennese Beguine: Life and Revelations, *Ulrike Wiethaus*, 2002

Women of the *Gilte Legende*: A Selection of Middle English Saints Lives, *Larissa Tracy*, 2003

Mechthild of Magdeburg: Selections from *The Flowing Light of the Godhead*, *Elizabeth A. Andersen*, 2003

The Book of Margery Kempe: An Abridged Translation, *Liz Herbert McAvoy*, 2003

Guidance for Women in Twelfth-Century Convents, *Vera Morton with Jocelyn Wogan-Browne*, 2003

Goscelin of St Bertin, *The Book of Encouragement and Consolation [Liber Confortatorius], Monika Otter*, 2004